FREE DVD FREE FREE DVD

From Stress to Success DVD from Trivium Test Prep

Dear Customer,

Thank you for purchasing from Trivium Test Prep! Whether you're looking to join the military, get into college, or advance your career, we're honored to be a part of your journey.

To show our appreciation (and to help you relieve a little of that test-prep stress), we're offering a **FREE *PERT Essential Test Tips DVD*** by Trivium Test Prep. Our DVD includes 35 test preparation strategies that will help keep you calm and collected before and during your big exam. All we ask is that you email us your feedback and describe your experience with our product. Amazing, awful, or just so-so: we want to hear what you have to say!

To receive your **FREE *PERT Essential Test Tips DVD***, please email us at 5star@triviumtestprep. com. Include "Free 5 Star" in the subject line and the following information in your email:

1. The title of the product you purchased.
2. Your rating from 1–5 (with 5 being the best).
3. Your feedback about the product, including how our materials helped you meet your goals and ways in which we can improve our products.
4. Your full name and shipping address so we can send your **FREE *PERT Essential Test Tips DVD***.

If you have any questions or concerns please feel free to contact us directly at 5star@triviumtestprep.com.

Thank you, and good luck with your studies!

PERT Study Guide 2021–2022

2021–2022

Exam Prep Review and Practice Questions for the Florida Postsecondary Education Readiness Test

TABLE OF CONTENTS

INTRODUCTION

Congratulations on choosing to take the PERT! By purchasing this book, you've taken the first step toward attending college. Understanding your academic strengths and weaknesses is crucial to succeeding at the college of your choice.

This guide will provide you with a detailed overview of the PERT so you know exactly what to expect on test day. We'll take you through all the concepts covered on the test and give you the opportunity to test your knowledge with practice questions. Even if it's been a while since you last took a major test, don't worry; we'll make sure you're more than ready!

WHAT IS THE PERT?

The PERT is a computer adaptive test established to determine whether a student is prepared for college level coursework. If a student does not meet the minimum required score set by the state, it's an indication that the student needs more academic preparation. The high school is then required to provide postsecondary preparatory instruction. All students enrolled in public high school in the state of Florida are required to take the PERT in the eleventh grade.

Any student who entered ninth grade in the 2003-04 academic year or after and earned a high school diploma from a Florida public school, or a student who is actively serving in a U.S. military branch is not required to enroll in developmental education instruction in a Florida College System institution.

WHAT'S ON THE PERT?

The PERT tests students' abilities in math, reading, and writing. The test directly tests for competence for intermediate algebra and freshman level composition. The PERT is not timed, and each section has thirty questions.

What's on the PERT?

SECTION	CONCEPTS
Math	Literal, linear, and quadratic equations; evaluating algebraic expressions, polynomials; dividing by monomials and binomials; applying standard algorithms; coordinate planes
Reading	Understanding the main idea; supporting/challenging assertions in text; determining the meaning of words and phrases in context; understanding the meaning, word choices, tone, and organizational structure of the text; determining the author's purpose; analyzing traits and motivations of characters; distinguishing fact and opinion; evaluating an arguement of the text
Writing	Establishing a topic or thesis; developing/maintaining style and tone; accurately citing data and opinions of others; supporting arguements; conveying complex information clearly; sentence structure skills; word choice skills; conceptual and organizational skills; grammar, spelling, capitalization, and punctuation skills

HOW IS THE PERT SCORED?

The PERT is not a test to pass or fail; it's used to determine the best academic path toward college for students. It's important for students to take the PERT seriously (even though it isn't graded) to ensure they are placed in the most appropriate classes.

The PERT is scored by section in a range of 50 – 150, with "cut scores" throughout (so students will get three different scores). There are three or four tiers (depending on the section) of cut scores to determine what level students are currently at.

Cut scores for the PERT

	SECTION	SCORE
MATH	Lower level developmental education	50 – 95
	Higher level developmental education	96 – 113
	Intermediate algebra	114* – 122
	College algebra or higher	123 – 150
READING	Lower level developmental education	50 – 83
	Higher level developmental education	84 – 105
	Freshman composition	106* – 150
WRITING	Lower level developmental education	50 – 89
	Higher level developmental education	90 – 102
	Freshman composition	103* – 150

Note: scores marked with an asterisk are the college-ready cut score.

HOW IS THE PERT ADMINISTERED?

The PERT is a computer adaptive test (CAT), meaning the test is administered electronically and questions are chosen based on answers to previous questions. Calculators are not permitted, but an onscreen calculator will pop-up for questions that require it. Students are not to change their answer once they have moved on to the next question. It is untimed so the student has as long as he or she needs to do well. The PERT is administered in school; at the end of the test, results are available immediately.

ABOUT TRIVIUM TEST PREP

Trivium Test Prep uses industry professionals with decades' worth of knowledge in their fields, proven with degrees and honors in law, medicine, business, education, the military, and more, to produce high-quality test prep books for students.

Our study guides are specifically designed to increase any student's score, regardless of his or her current skill level. Our books are also shorter and more concise than typical study guides, so you can increase your score while significantly decreasing your study time.

HOW TO USE THIS GUIDE

This guide is not meant to waste your time on superfluous information or concepts you've already learned. Instead, this guide will help you master the most important test topics and also develop critical test-taking skills. To support this effort, the guide provides:

- organized concepts with detailed explanations
- practice questions with worked-through solutions
- key test-taking strategies
- simulated one-on-one tutor experience
- tips, tricks, and test secrets

Because we have eliminated the filler and fluff, you'll be able to work through the guide at a significantly faster pace than you would with other test prep books. By allowing you to focus only on those concepts that will increase your score, we'll make your study time shorter and more effective.

Now that you have a firm understanding of the exam and what is included our book, don't forget that learning how to study, as well as how to successfully pass an exam, is just as important as the content. Trivium Test Prep would like to remind you as you begin your studies that we are offering a **FREE *From Stress to Success* DVD**. Our DVD includes 35 test preparation strategies that will help keep you calm and collected before and during your big exam. All we ask is that you email us your feedback and describe your experience with our product. Amazing, awful, or just so-so: we want to hear what you have to say!

To receive your **FREE *From Stress to Success* DVD**, please email us at 5star@triviumtestprep. com. Include

"Free 5 Star" in the subject line and the following information in your email:

1. The title of the product you purchased.
2. Your rating from 1 – 5 (with 5 being the best).
3. Your feedback about the product, including how our materials helped you meet your goals and ways in which we can improve our products.
4. Your full name and shipping address so we can send your **FREE *From Stress to Success* DVD**.

We hope you find the rest of this study guide helpful.

MATHEMATICS

The PERT Mathematics section covers high-school level topics including basic operations, like order of operations and percentages, and algebra, including solving equations and expressions. The section includes thirty multiple-choice questions.

MATHEMATICS STRATEGIES

Go Back to the Basics

First and foremost, practice your basic skills: sign changes, order of operations, simplifying fractions, and equation manipulation. These are the skills used most on the PERT, though they are applied in different contexts. Remember that when it comes down to it, all math problems rely on the four basic skills of addition, subtraction, multiplication, and division. All you need to figure out is the order in which they're used to solve a problem.

Don't Rely on Mental Math

Using mental math is great for eliminating answer choices, but ALWAYS WRITE DOWN YOUR WORK! This cannot be stressed enough. Use whatever paper is provided; by writing and/or drawing out the problem, you are more likely to catch any mistakes.

The Three-Times Rule

You should read each question at least three times to ensure you're using the correct information and answering the right question:

> Step One: Read the question and write out the given information.

> Step Two: Read the question, set up your equation(s), and solve.

Step Three: Read the question and check that your answer makes sense (is the amount too large or small; is the answer in the correct unit of measurement, etc.).

Make an Educated Guess

Eliminate those answer choices which you are relatively sure are incorrect, and then guess from the remaining choices. Educated guessing is critical to increasing your score.

TYPES OF NUMBERS

INTEGERS are whole numbers, including the counting numbers, the negative counting numbers and zero. 3, 2, 1, 0, −1, −2, −3 are examples of integers. RATIONAL NUMBERS are made by dividing one integer by another integer. They can be expressed as fractions or as decimals. 3 divided by 4 makes the rational number $\frac{3}{4}$ or 0.75. IRRATIONAL NUMBERS are numbers that cannot be written as fractions; they are decimals that go on forever without repeating. The number π (3.14159…) is an example of an irrational number.

IMAGINARY NUMBERS are numbers that, when squared, give a negative result. Imaginary numbers use the symbol i to represent $\sqrt{-1}$, so $3i = \sqrt[3]{-1}$ and $(3i)^2 = -9$. COMPLEX NUMBERS are combinations of real and imaginary numbers, written in the form $a + bi$, where a is the real number and b is the imaginary number. An example of a complex number is $4 + 2i$. When adding complex numbers, add the real and imaginary numbers separately: $(4 + 2i) + (3 + i) = 7 + 3i$.

Examples

1. Is $\sqrt{5}$ a rational or irrational number?

   $\sqrt{5}$ **is an irrational number** because it cannot be written as a fraction of two integers. It is a decimal that goes on forever without repeating.

2. What kind of number is $-\sqrt{64}$?

   $-\sqrt{64}$ can be rewritten as the negative whole number −8, so **it is an integer.**

3. Solve $(3 + 5i) - (1 - 2i)$

   Subtract the real and imaginary numbers separately.

   $3 - 1 = 2$

   $5i - (-2i) = 5i + 2i = 7i$

   $(3 + 5i) - (1 - 2i) =$

   $2 + 7i$

POSITIVE AND NEGATIVE NUMBERS

Adding, multiplying, and dividing numbers can yield positive or negative values depending on the signs of the original numbers. Knowing these rules can help determine if your answer is correct.

$(+) + (-) =$ the sign of the larger number

$(-) + (-) =$ negative number

$(-) \times (-) =$ positive number

$(-) \times (+) =$ negative number

$(-) \div (-) =$ positive number

$(-) \div (+) =$ negative number

Examples

1. Find the product of −10 and 47.

$(-) \times (+) = (-)$

$-10 \times 47 =$ **−470**

2. What is the sum of −65 and −32?

$(-) + (-) = (-)$

$-65 + -32 =$ **−97**

3. Is the product of −7 and 4 less than −7, between −7 and 4, or greater than 4?

$(-) \times (+) = (-)$

$-7 \times 4 = -28$, which is **less than −7**

4. What is the value of −16 divided by 2.5?

$(-) \div (+) = (-)$

$-16 \div 2.5 =$ **−6.4**

ORDER OF OPERATIONS

Operations in a mathematical expression are always performed in a specific order, which is described by the acronym PEMDAS:

1. Parentheses

2. Exponents

3. Multiplication

4. Division

5. Addition

6. Subtraction

Perform the operations within parentheses first, and then address any exponents. After those steps, perform all multiplication and division. These are carried out from left to right as they appear in the problem.

Finally, do all required addition and subtraction, also from left to right as each operation appears in the problem.

Examples

1. Solve: $[-(2)^2 - (4 + 7)]$

   First, complete operations within parentheses:

   $-(2)^2 - (11)$

   Second, calculate the value of exponential numbers:

   $-(4) - (11)$

   Finally, do addition and subtraction:

   $-4 - 11 = \mathbf{-15}$

2. Solve: $(5)^2 \div 5 + 4 \times 2$

   First, calculate the value of exponential numbers:

   $(25) \div 5 + 4 \times 2$

   Second, calculate division and multiplication from left to right:

   $5 + 8$

   Finally, do addition and subtraction:

   $5 + 8 = \mathbf{13}$

3. Solve the expression: $15 \times (4 + 8) - 3^3$

   First, complete operations within parentheses:

   $15 \times (12) - 3^3$

   Second, calculate the value of exponential numbers:

   $15 \times (12) - 27$

   Third, calculate division and multiplication from left to right:

   $180 - 27$

   Finally, do addition and subtraction from left to right:

   $180 - 27 = \mathbf{153}$

4. Solve the expression: $\left(\frac{5}{2} \times 4\right) + 23 - 4^2$

   First, complete operations within parentheses:

   $(10) + 23 - 4^2$

   Second, calculate the value of exponential numbers:

   $(10) + 23 - 16$

   Finally, do addition and subtraction from left to right:

   $(10) + 23 - 16$

   $33 - 16 = \mathbf{17}$

UNITS OF MEASUREMENT

You are expected to memorize some units of measurement. These are given below. When doing unit conversion problems (i.e., when converting one unit to another), find the conversion factor, then apply that factor to the given measurement to find the new units.

Table 1.1. Unit prefixes

PREFIX	SYMBOL	MULTIPLICATION FACTOR
tera	T	1,000,000,000,000
giga	G	1,000,000,000
mega	M	1,000,000
kilo	k	1,000
hecto	h	100
deca	da	10
base unit	--	--
deci	d	0.1
centi	c	0.01
milli	m	0.001
micro	μ	0.0000001
nano	n	0.0000000001
pico	p	0.0000000000001

Table 1.2. Units and conversion factors

DIMENSION	AMERICAN	SI
length	inch/foot/yard/mile	meter
mass	ounce/pound/ton	gram
volume	cup/pint/quart/gallon	liter
force	pound-force	newton
pressure	pound-force per square inch	pascal
work and energy	cal/British thermal unit	joule
temperature	Fahrenheit	kelvin
charge	faraday	coulomb

CONVERSION FACTORS

1 in = 2.54 cm	1 lb = 0.454 kg
1 yd = 0.914 m	1 cal = 4.19 J
1 mi = 1.61 km	1 °F = 5/9 (°F − 32)
1 gal = 3.785 L	1 cm³ = 1 mL
1 oz = 28.35 g	1 hr = 3600 s

Examples

1. A fence measures 15 ft. long. How many yards long is the fence?

   1 yd. = 3 ft.

   $\frac{15}{3}$ = **5 yd.**

CONTINUE →

2. A pitcher can hold 24 cups. How many gallons can it hold?

1 gal. = 16 cups

$\frac{24}{16}$ = **1.5 gallons**

3. A spool of wire holds 144 in. of wire. If Mario has 3 spools, how many feet of wire does he have?

12 in. = 1 ft.

$\frac{144}{12}$ = 12 ft.

12 ft. × 3 spools = **36 ft. of wire**

4. A ball rolling across a table travels 6 inches per second. How many feet will it travel in 1 minute?

This problem can be worked in two steps: finding how many inches are covered in 1 minute, and then converting that value to feet. It can also be worked the opposite way, by finding how many feet it travels in 1 second and then converting that to feet traveled per minute. The first method is shown below.

1 min. = 60 sec.

(6 in.)/(sec.) × 60 s = 360 in.

1 ft. = 12 in.

(360 in.)/(12 in.) = **30 ft.**

5. How many millimeters are in 0.5 m?

1 meter = 1000 mm

0.5 meters = **500 mm**

6. A lead ball weighs 38 g. How many kilograms does it weigh?

1 kg = 1000 g

$\frac{38}{1000}$ g = **0.038 kg**

7. How many cubic centimeters are in 10 L?

1 L = 1000

10 L = 1000 × 10

10 L = **10,000**

8. Jennifer's pencil was initially 10 centimeters long. After she sharpened it, it was 9.6 centimeters long. How many millimeters did she lose from her pencil by sharpening it?

1 cm = 10 mm

10 cm − 9.6 cm = 0.4 cm lost

0.4 cm = 10 × .4 mm = **4 mm were lost**

DECIMALS AND FRACTIONS

Adding and Subtracting Decimals

When adding and subtracting decimals, line up the numbers so that the decimals are aligned. You want to subtract the ones place from the ones place, the tenths place from the tenths place, etc.

Examples

1. Find the sum of 17.07 and 2.52.

$$
\begin{array}{r}
17.07 \\
+\ \ 2.52 \\
\hline
=\mathbf{19.59}
\end{array}
$$

2. Jeannette has 7.4 gallons of gas in her tank. After driving, she has 6.8 gallons. How many gallons of gas did she use?

$$
\begin{array}{r}
7.4 \\
-\ 6.8 \\
\hline
=\mathbf{0.6\ gal.}
\end{array}
$$

Multiplying and Dividing Decimals

When multiplying decimals, start by multiplying the numbers normally. You can then determine the placement of the decimal point in the result by adding the number of digits after the decimal in each of the numbers you multiplied together.

When dividing decimals, you should move the decimal point in the divisor (the number you're dividing by) until it is a whole. You can then move the decimal in the dividend (the number you're dividing into) the same number of places in the same direction. Finally, divide the new numbers normally to get the correct answer.

Examples

1. What is the product of 0.25 and 1.4?

   $25 \times 14 = 350$

   There are 2 digits after the decimal in 0.25 and one digit after the decimal in 1.4. Therefore the product should have 3 digits after the decimal: **0.350** is the correct answer.

2. Find $0.8 \div 0.2$.

   Change 0.2 to 2 by moving the decimal one space to the right.

   Next, move the decimal one space to the right on the dividend. 0.8 becomes 8.

   Now, divide 8 by 2. $8 \div 2 = \mathbf{4}$

3. Find the quotient when 40 is divided by 0.25.

First, change the divisor to a whole number: 0.25 becomes 25.

Next, change the dividend to match the divisor by moving the decimal two spaces to the right, so 40 becomes 4000.

Now divide: 4000 ÷ 25 = **160**

Working with Fractions

FRACTIONS are made up of two parts: the NUMERATOR, which appears above the bar, and the DENOMINATOR, which is below it. If a fraction is in its SIMPLEST FORM, the numerator and the denominator share no common factors. A fraction with a numerator larger than its denominator is an IMPROPER FRACTION; when the denominator is larger, it's a PROPER FRACTION.

Improper fractions can be converted into proper fractions by dividing the numerator by the denominator. The resulting whole number is placed to the left of the fraction, and the remainder becomes the new numerator; the denominator does not change. The new number is called a MIXED NUMBER because it contains a whole number and a fraction. Mixed numbers can be turned into improper fractions through the reverse process: multiply the whole number by the denominator and add the numerator to get the new numerator.

Examples

1. Simplify the fraction $\frac{121}{77}$.

121 and 77 share a common factor of 11. So, if we divide each by 11 we can simplify the fraction:

$$\frac{121}{77} = \frac{11}{11} \times \frac{11}{7} = \frac{11}{7}$$

2. Convert $\frac{37}{5}$ into a proper fraction.

Start by dividing the numerator by the denominator:

$37 \div 5 = 7$ with a remainder of 2

Now build a mixed number with the whole number and the new numerator:

$$\frac{37}{5} = 7\frac{2}{5}$$

Multiplying and Dividing Fractions

To multiply fractions, convert any mixed numbers into improper fractions and multiply the numerators together and the denominators together. Reduce to lowest terms if needed.

To divide fractions, first convert any mixed fractions into single fractions. Then, invert the second fraction so that the denominator and numerator are switched. Finally, multiply the numerators together and the denominators together.

Inverting a fraction changes multiplication to division:
$\frac{a}{b} \div \frac{c}{d} = \frac{a}{b} \times \frac{d}{c} = \frac{ad}{bc}$

Examples

1. What is the product of $\frac{1}{12}$ and $\frac{6}{8}$?

Simply multiply the numerators together and the denominators together, then reduce:

$$\frac{1}{12} \times \frac{6}{8} = \frac{6}{96} = \mathbf{\frac{1}{16}}$$

Sometimes it's easier to reduce fractions before multiplying if you can:

$$\frac{1}{12} \times \frac{6}{8} = \frac{1}{12} \times \frac{3}{4} = \frac{3}{48} = \mathbf{\frac{1}{16}}$$

2. Find $\frac{7}{8} \div \frac{1}{4}$.

For a fraction division problem, invert the second fraction and then multiply and reduce:

$$\frac{7}{8} \div \frac{1}{4} = \frac{7}{8} \times \frac{4}{1} = \frac{28}{8} = \mathbf{\frac{7}{2}}$$

The quotient is the result you get when you divide two numbers.

3. What is the quotient of $\frac{2}{5} \div 1\frac{1}{5}$?

This is a fraction division problem, so the first step is to convert the mixed number to an improper fraction:

$$1\frac{1}{5} = \frac{5 \times 1}{5} + \frac{1}{5} = \frac{6}{5}$$

Now, divide the fractions. Remember to invert the second fraction, and then multiply normally:

$$\frac{2}{5} \div \frac{6}{5} = \frac{2}{5} \times \frac{5}{6} = \frac{10}{30} = \mathbf{\frac{1}{3}}$$

4. A recipe calls for $\frac{1}{4}$ cup of sugar. If 8.5 batches of the recipe are needed, how many cups of sugar will be used?

This is a fraction multiplication problem: $\frac{1}{4} \times 8\frac{1}{2}$.

First, we need to convert the mixed number into a proper fraction:

$$8\frac{1}{2} = \frac{8 \times 2}{2} + \frac{1}{2} = \frac{17}{2}$$

Now, multiply the fractions across the numerators and denominators, and then reduce:

$$\frac{1}{4} \times 8\frac{1}{2} = \frac{1}{4} \times \frac{17}{2} = \mathbf{\frac{17}{8}} \textbf{ cups of sugar}$$

Adding and Subtracting Fractions

Adding and subtracting fractions requires a **COMMON DENOMINATOR**. To find the common denominator, you can multiply each fraction by the number 1. With fractions, any number over itself (e.g., $\frac{5}{5}$, $\frac{12}{12}$, etc.) is equivalent to 1, so multiplying by such a fraction can change the denominator without changing the value of the fraction. Once the denominators are the same, the numerators can be added or subtracted.

CONTINUE

To add mixed numbers, you can first add the whole numbers and then the fractions. To subtract mixed numbers, convert each number to an improper fraction, then subtract the numerators.

The phrase *simplify the expression* just means you need to perform all the operations in the expression.

Examples

1. Simplify the expression $\frac{2}{3} - \frac{1}{5}$.

   First, multiply each fraction by a factor of 1 to get a common denominator. How do you know which factor of 1 to use? Look at the other fraction and use the number found in that denominator:

   $$\frac{2}{3} - \frac{1}{5} = \frac{2}{3}\left(\frac{5}{5}\right) - \frac{1}{5}\left(\frac{3}{3}\right) = \frac{10}{15} - \frac{3}{15}$$

   Once the fractions have a common denominator, simply subtract the numerators:

   $$\frac{10}{15} - \frac{3}{15} = \frac{7}{15}$$

2. Find $2\frac{1}{3} - \frac{3}{2}$.

   This is a problem with a mixed number, so the first step is to convert the mixed number to an improper fraction:

   $$2\frac{1}{3} = \frac{2 \times 3}{3} + \frac{1}{3} = \frac{7}{3}$$

   Next, convert each fraction so they share a common denominator:

   $$\frac{7}{3} \times \frac{2}{2} = \frac{14}{6}$$

   $$\frac{3}{2} \times \frac{3}{3} = \frac{9}{6}$$

   Now, subtract the fractions by subtracting the numerators:

   $$\frac{14}{6} - \frac{9}{6} = \frac{5}{6}$$

3. Find the sum of $\frac{9}{16}, \frac{1}{2}$, and $\frac{7}{4}$.

   For this fraction addition problem, we need to find a common denominator. Notice that 2 and 4 are both factors of 16, so 16 can be the common denominator:

   $$\frac{1}{2} \times \frac{8}{8} = \frac{8}{16}$$

   $$\frac{7}{4} \times \frac{4}{4} = \frac{28}{16}$$

   $$\frac{9}{16} + \frac{8}{16} + \frac{28}{16} = \frac{45}{16}$$

4. Sabrina has $\frac{2}{3}$ of a can of red paint. Her friend Amos has $\frac{1}{6}$ of a can. How much red paint do they have combined?

   To add fractions, make sure that they have a common denominator. Since 3 is a factor of 6, 6 can be the common denominator:

   $$\frac{2}{3} \times \frac{2}{2} = \frac{4}{6}$$

   Now, add the numerators:

   $$\frac{4}{6} + \frac{1}{6} = \frac{5}{6} \text{ of a can}$$

Converting Fractions to Decimals

Calculators are not allowed on the PERT, which can make handling fractions and decimals intimidating for many test-takers. However, there are several techniques you can use to help you convert between the two forms.

The first thing to do is simply memorize common decimals and their fractional equivalents; a list of these is given below. With these values, it's possible to convert more complicated fractions as well. For example, $\frac{2}{5}$ is just $\frac{1}{5}$ multiplied by 2, so $\frac{2}{5} = 0.2 \times 2 = 0.4$.

Table 1.3. Common decimals and fractions

FRACTION	DECIMAL
$\frac{1}{2}$	0.5
$\frac{1}{3}$	$0.\overline{33}$
$\frac{1}{4}$	0.25
$\frac{1}{5}$	0.2
$\frac{1}{6}$	$0.1\overline{66}$
$\frac{1}{7}$	$0.\overline{142857}$
$\frac{1}{8}$	0.125
$\frac{1}{9}$	$0.\overline{11}$
$\frac{1}{10}$	0.1

Knowledge of common decimal equivalents to fractions can also help you estimate. This skill can be particularly helpful on multiple-choice tests like the PERT, where excluding incorrect answers can be just as helpful as knowing how to find the right one. For example, to find in decimal form for an answer, you can eliminate any answers less than 0.5 because $\frac{4}{8} = 0.5$. You may also know that $\frac{6}{8}$ is the same as $\frac{3}{4}$ or 0.75, so anything above 0.75 can be eliminated as well.

Another helpful trick can be used if the denominator is easily divisible by 100: in the fraction $\frac{9}{20}$, you know 20 goes into 100 five times, so you can multiply the top and bottom by 5 to get $\frac{45}{100}$ or 0.45.

If none of these techniques work, you'll need to find the decimal by dividing the denominator by the numerator using long division.

$\longrightarrow$
CONTINUE

Examples

1. Write $\frac{8}{18}$ as a decimal.

   The first step here is to simplify the fraction:

   $$\frac{8}{18} = \frac{4}{9}$$

   Now it's clear that the fraction is a multiple of $\frac{1}{9}$, so you can easily find the decimal using a value you already know:

   $$\frac{4}{9} = \frac{1}{9} \times 4 = 0.\overline{11} \times 4 = \mathbf{0.\overline{44}}$$

2. Write the fraction $\frac{3}{16}$ as a decimal.

   None of the tricks above will work for this fraction, so you need to do long division:

   ```
          0.1875
     16 ⟌ 3.0000
        − 1 6
          1 40
        − 1 28
            120
        −   112
             80
        −    80
              0
   ```

   $$\frac{3}{16} = \mathbf{0.1875}$$

Converting Decimals to Fractions

Converting a decimal into a fraction is more straightforward than the reverse process. To convert a decimal, simply use the numbers that come after the decimal as the numerator in the fraction. The denominator will be a power of 10 that matches the place value for the original decimal. For example, the numerator for 0.46 would be 100 because the last number is in the tenths place; likewise, the denominator for 0.657 would be 1000 because the last number is in the thousandths place. Once this fraction has been set up, all that's left is to simplify it.

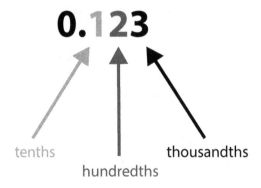

Figure 1.1. Simplified decimal

Example

Convert 0.45 into a fraction.

The last number in the decimal is in the hundredths place, so we can easily set up a fraction:

$0.45 = \frac{45}{100}$

The next step is to simply reduce the fraction down to the lowest common denominator. Here, both 45 and 100 are divisible by 5: 45 divided by 5 is 9, and 100 divided by 5 is 20. Therefore, you're left with:

$\frac{45}{100} = \mathbf{\frac{9}{20}}$

RATIOS

A **RATIO** tells you how many of one thing exists in relation to the number of another thing. Unlike fractions, ratios do not give a part relative to a whole; instead, they compare two values. For example, if you have 3 apples and 4 oranges, the ratio of apples to oranges is 3 to 4. Ratios can be written using words (3 to 4), fractions ($\frac{3}{4}$), or colons (3:4).

In order to work with ratios, it's helpful to rewrite them as a fraction expressing a part to a whole. For example, in the example above you have 7 total pieces of fruit, so the fraction of your fruit that are apples is $\frac{3}{7}$, and oranges make up $\frac{4}{7}$ of your fruit collection.

One last important thing to consider when working with ratios is the units of the values being compared. On the PERT, you may be asked to rewrite a ratio using the same units on both sides. For example, you might have to rewrite the ratio 3 minutes to 7 seconds as 180 seconds to 7 seconds.

Examples

1. There are 90 voters in a room, and each is either a Democrat or a Republican. The ratio of Democrats to Republicans is 5:4. How many Republicans are there?

   We know that there are 5 Democrats for every 4 Republicans in the room, which means for every 9 people, 4 are Republicans.

   $5 + 4 = 9$

   Fraction of Democrats: $\frac{5}{9}$

   Fraction of Republicans: $\frac{4}{9}$

   If $\frac{4}{9}$ of the 90 voters are Republicans, then:

   $\frac{4}{9} \times 90 = $ **40 voters are Republicans**

CONTINUE

2. The ratio of students to teachers in a school is 15:1. If there are 38 teachers, how many students attend the school?

To solve this ratio problem, we can simply multiply both sides of the ratio by the desired value to find the number of students that correspond to having 38 teachers:

$$\frac{15 \text{ students}}{1 \text{ teacher}} \times \frac{38}{38} = \frac{570 \text{ students}}{38 \text{ teachers}}$$

The school has 570 students.

Ratio and proportion problems are among the most common on the PERT.

PROPORTIONS

A **PROPORTION** is an equation which states that 2 ratios are equal. Proportions are usually written as 2 fractions joined by an equal sign $\left(\frac{a}{b} = \frac{c}{d}\right)$, but they can also be written using colons (a : b :: c : d). Note that in a proportion, the units must be the same in both numerators and in both denominators.

Often you will be given 3 of the values in a proportion and asked to find the 4th. In these types of problems, you can solve for the missing variable by cross-multiplying—multiply the numerator of each fraction by the denominator of the other to get an equation with no fractions as shown below. You can then solve the equation using basic algebra.

$$\frac{a}{b} = \frac{c}{d} \rightarrow ad = bc$$

Examples

1. A train traveling 120 miles takes 3 hours to get to its destination. How long will it take for the train to travel 180 miles?

Start by setting up the proportion:

$$\frac{120 \text{ mi.}}{3 \text{ hr.}} = \frac{180 \text{ mi.}}{x \text{ hr.}}$$

Note that it doesn't matter which value is placed in the numerator or denominator, as long as it is the same on both sides. Now, solve for the missing quantity through cross–multiplication:

120 mi. × x hr. = 3 hr. × 180 mi.

Now solve the equation:

$$x \text{ hr.} = \frac{(3 \text{ hr.}) \times (180 \text{ mi.})}{120 \text{ mi.}} = \textbf{4.5 hr.}$$

2. One acre of wheat requires 500 gallons of water. How many acres can be watered with 2600 gallons?

Set up the equation:

$$\frac{1 \text{ acre}}{500 \text{ gal.}} = \frac{x \text{ acres}}{2600 \text{ gal.}}$$

Then solve for x:

$$x \text{ acres} = \frac{1 \text{ acre} \times 2600 \text{ gal.}}{500 \text{ gal.}}$$

$$x = \frac{26}{5} \text{ or } \textbf{5.2 acres}$$

3. If $35 : 5 :: 49 : x$, find x.

   This problem presents two equivalent ratios that can be set up in a fraction equation:

   $$\frac{35}{5} = \frac{49}{x}$$

   You can then cross-multiply to solve for x:

   $$35x = 49 \times 5$$

   $$\boldsymbol{x = 7}$$

PERCENTAGES

A PERCENT is the ratio of a part to the whole. Questions may give the part and the whole and ask for the percent, or give the percent and the whole and ask for the part, or give the part and the percent and ask for the value of the whole. The equation for percentages can be rearranged to solve for any of these:

$$percent = \frac{part}{whole}$$

$$part = whole \times percent$$

$$whole = \frac{part}{percent}$$

In the equations above, the percent should always be expressed as a decimal. In order to convert a decimal into a percentage value, simply multiply it by 100. So, If you've read 5 pages (the part) of a 10 page article (the whole), you've read $\frac{5}{10} = 0.5$ or 50%. (The percent sign (%) is used once the decimal has been multiplied by 100.)

Note that when solving these problems, the units for the part and the whole should be the same. If you're reading a book, saying you've read 5 pages out of 15 chapters doesn't make any sense.

The word *of* usually indicates what the whole is in a problem. For example, the problem might say *Ella ate 2 slices of the pizza*, which means the pizza is the whole.

Examples

1. 45 is 15% of what number?

   Set up the appropriate equation and solve. Don't forget to change 15% to a decimal value:

   $$whole = \frac{part}{percent} = \frac{45}{0.15} = \textbf{300}$$

2. Jim spent 30% of his paycheck at the fair. He spent $15 for a hat, $30 for a shirt, and $20 playing games. How much was his check? (Round to nearest dollar.)

   Set up the appropriate equation and solve:

   $$whole = \frac{part}{percent} = \frac{15 + 30 + 20}{.30} = \textbf{\$217.00}$$

3. What percent of 65 is 39?

Set up the equation and solve:

$percent = \frac{part}{whole} = \frac{39}{65} = 0.6$ or **60%**

4. Parvarti and Mario sell cable subscriptions. In a given month, Parvarti sells 45 subscriptions and Mario sells 51. If 240 total subscriptions were sold in that month, what percent were not sold by Parvarti or Mario?

You can use the information in the question to figure out what percentage of subscriptions were sold by Parvarti and Mario:

$percent = \frac{part}{whole} = 51 + \frac{45}{240} = 0.4$ or 40%

However, the question asks how many subscriptions weren't sold by Mario or Parvarti. If they sold 40%, then the other salespeople sold $100\% - 40\% = $ **60%**.

5. Grant needs to score 75% on an exam. If the exam has 45 questions, at least how many does he need to answer correctly?

Set up the equation and solve. Remember to convert 75% to a decimal value:

$part = whole \times percent = 45 \times 0.75 = 33.75$, so he needs to answer **at least 34 questions correctly.**

Percent Change

Percent change problems will ask you to calculate how much a given quantity changed. The problems are solved in a similar way as regular percent problems, except that instead of using the *part* you'll use the *amount of change*. Note that the sign of the *amount of change* is important: if the original amount has increased the change will be positive, and if it has decreased the change will be negative. Again, in the equations below the percent is a decimal value; you need to multiply by 100 to get the actual percentage.

$$percent\ change = \frac{amount\ of\ change}{original\ amount}$$

$$amount\ of\ change = original\ amount \times percent\ change$$

$$original\ amount = \frac{amount\ of\ change}{percent\ change}$$

Examples

1. A computer software retailer marks up its games by 40% above the wholesale price when it sells them to customers. Find the price of a game for a customer if the game cost the retailer $25.

Set up the appropriate equation and solve:

amount of change = original amount × percent change

$10 = 25 \times 0.4$

If the amount of change is 10, that means the store adds a markup of $10, so the game costs:

$25 + $10 = **$35**

2. A golf shop pays its wholesaler $40 for a certain club, and then sells it to a golfer for $75. What is the markup rate?

First, calculate the amount of change:

75 − 40 = 35

Now you can set up the equation and solve. (Note that *markup rate* is another way of saying *percent change*):

$percent\ change = \dfrac{amount\ of\ change}{original\ amount} = \dfrac{35}{40} = 0.875 = $ **87.5%**

3. A store charges a 40% markup on the shoes it sells. How much did the store pay for a pair of shoes purchased by a customer for $63?

You're solving for the original price, but it's going to be tricky because you don't know the amount of change; you only know the new price. To solve, you need to create an expression for the amount of change:

If *original amount* = x

Then *amount of change* = 63 − x

Now you can plug these values into your equation:

original amount = *amount of change* ÷ *percent change*

$x = \dfrac{63 - x}{0.4}$

The last step is to solve for x:

$0.4x = 63 - x$

$1.4x = 63$

$x = 45$

The store paid $45 for the shoes.

4. An item originally priced at $55 is marked 25% off. What is the sale price?

You've been asked to find the sale price, which means you need to solve for the amount of change first:

amount of change = *original amount* × *percent change*

$= 55 \times 0.25 = 13.75$

Using this amount, you can find the new price. Because it's on sale, we know the item will cost less than the original price:

55 − 13.75 = 41.25

The sale price is $41.25.

5. James wants to put in an 18 foot by 51 foot garden in his backyard. If he does, it will reduce the size of his yard by 24%. What will be the area of the remaining yard?

CONTINUE

This problem is tricky because you need to figure out what each number in the problem stands for. 24% is obviously the percent change, but what about the measurements in feet? If you multiply these values you get the area of the garden (for more on area see *Area and Perimeter*):

18 ft. × 51 ft. = 918 ft.²

This 918 ft.² is the amount of change—it's how much smaller the lawn is. Now we can set up an equation:

$$original\ amount = \frac{amount\ of\ change}{percent\ change} = \frac{918}{24} = 3825$$

If the original lawn was 3825 ft.² and the garden is 918 ft.², then the remaining area is

3825 – 918 = 2907

The remaining lawn covers **2907 ft.²**

COMPARISON OF RATIONAL NUMBERS

Number comparison problems present numbers in different formats and ask which is larger or smaller, or whether the numbers are equivalent. The important step in solving these problems is to convert the numbers to the same format so that it is easier to compare them. If numbers are given in the same format, or after converting them, determine which number is smaller or if the numbers are equal. Remember that for negative numbers, higher numbers are actually smaller.

Examples

1. Is $4\frac{3}{4}$ greater than, equal to, or less than $\frac{18}{4}$?

   These numbers are in different formats—one is a mixed fraction and the other is just a fraction. So, the first step is to convert the mixed fraction to a fraction:

   $$4\frac{3}{4} = 4 \times \frac{4}{4} + \frac{3}{4} = \frac{19}{4}$$

   Once the mixed number is converted, it is easier to see that $\frac{19}{4}$ **is greater than** $\frac{18}{4}$.

2. Which of the following numbers has the greatest value: 104.56, 104.5, or 104.6?

   These numbers are already in the same format, so the decimal values just need to be compared. Remember that zeros can be added after the decimal without changing the value, so the three numbers can be rewritten as:

   104.56

   104.50

   104.60

   From this list, it is clearer to see that **104.60 is the greatest** because 0.60 is larger than 0.50 and 0.56.

3. Is 65% greater than, less than, or equal to $\frac{13}{20}$?

The first step is to convert the numbers into the same format. 65% is the same as $\frac{65}{100}$. Next, the fractions need to be converted to have the same denominator. It is difficult to compare fractions with different denominators. Using a factor of $\frac{5}{5}$ on the second fraction will give common denominators:

$\frac{13}{20} \times \frac{5}{5} = \frac{65}{100}$.

Now, it is easy to see that **the numbers are equivalent.**

EXPONENTS AND RADICALS

Exponents tell us how many times to multiply a base number by itself. In the example 2^4, 2 is the base number and 4 is the exponent. $2^4 = 2 \times 2 \times 2 \times 2 = 16$. Exponents are also called powers: 5 to the third power $= 5^3 = 5 \times 5 \times 5 = 125$. Some exponents have special names: x to the second power is also called "x squared" and x to the third power is also called "x cubed." The number 3 squared $= 3^2 = 3 \times 3 = 9$.

Radicals are expressions that use roots. Radicals are written in the form $\sqrt{(a \ \& \ x)}$, where a = the radical power and x = the radicand. The solution to the radical $\sqrt[3]{8}$ is the number that, when multiplied by itself 3 times, equals 8. $\sqrt[3]{8} = 2$ because $2 \times 2 \times 2 = 8$. When the radical power is not written we assume it is 2, so $\sqrt{9} = 3$ because $3 \times 3 = 9$. Radicals can also be written as exponents, where the power is a fraction. For example, $x^{\frac{1}{3}} = \sqrt[3]{x}$.

Review more of the rules for working with exponents and radicals in the table below.

Table 1.4. Exponents and radicals rules

RULE	EXAMPLE
$x^0 = 1$	$5^0 = 1$
$x^1 = x$	$5^1 = 5$
$x^a \times x^b = x^{a+b}$	$5^2 \times 5^3 = 5^5 = 3125$
$(xy)^a = x^a y^a$	$(5 \times 6)^2 = 5^2 \times 6^2 = 900$
$(x^a)^b = x^{ab}$	$(5^2)^3 = 5^6 = 15,625$
$\left(\frac{x}{y}\right)^a = \frac{x^a}{y^b}$	$\left(\frac{5}{6}\right)^2 = \frac{5^2}{6^2} = \frac{25}{36}$
$\frac{x^a}{x^b} = x^{a-b} \ (x \neq 0)$	$\frac{5^4}{5^3} = 5^1 = 5$
$x^{-a} = \frac{1}{x^a} \ (x \neq 0)$	$5^{-2} = \frac{1}{5^2} = \frac{1}{25}$

$$x^{\frac{1}{a}} = \sqrt[a]{x} \qquad\qquad 25^{\frac{1}{2}} = \sqrt[2]{25} = 5$$

$$\sqrt[a]{x \times y} = \sqrt[a]{x} \times \sqrt[a]{y} \qquad \sqrt[3]{8 \times 27} = \sqrt[3]{8} \times \sqrt[3]{27} = 2 \times 3 = 6$$

$$\sqrt[a]{\frac{x}{y}} = \frac{\sqrt[a]{x}}{\sqrt[a]{y}} \qquad\qquad \sqrt[3]{\frac{27}{8}} = \frac{\sqrt[3]{27}}{\sqrt[3]{8}} = \frac{3}{2}$$

$$\sqrt[a]{x^b} = x^{\frac{b}{a}} \qquad\qquad \sqrt[2]{5^4} = 5^{\frac{4}{2}} = 5^2 = 25$$

Examples

1. Simplify the expression $2^4 \times 2^2$

   When multiplying exponents in which the base number is the same, simply add the powers:

   $2^4 \times 2^2 = 2^{(4+2)} = 2^6$

   $2^6 = 2 \times 2 \times 2 \times 2 \times 2 \times 2 = \mathbf{64}$

2. Simplify the expression $(3^4)^{-1}$

   When an exponent is raised to a power, multiply the powers:

   $(3^4)^{-1} = 3^{-4}$

   When the exponent is a negative number, rewrite as the reciprocal of the positive exponent:

   $3^{-4} = \frac{1}{3^4}$

   $\frac{1}{3^4} = \frac{1}{3 \times 3 \times 3 \times 3} = \mathbf{\frac{1}{81}}$

3. Simplify the expression $\left(\frac{9}{4}\right)^{\frac{1}{2}}$

   When the power is a fraction, rewrite as a radical:

   $\left(\frac{9}{4}\right)^{\frac{1}{2}} = \sqrt{\frac{9}{4}}$

   Next, distribute the radical to the numerator and denominator:

   $\sqrt{\frac{9}{4}} = \frac{\sqrt{9}}{\sqrt{4}} = \mathbf{\frac{3}{2}}$

ALGEBRAIC EXPRESSIONS

Algebraic expressions and equations include VARIABLES, or letters standing in for numbers. These expressions and equations are made up of terms, which are groups of numbers and variables (e.g., $2xy$). An EXPRESSION is simply a set of terms (e.g., $\frac{2x}{3yz} + 2$). When those terms are joined only by addition or subtraction, the expression is called a POLYNOMIAL (e.g., $2x + 3yz$). When working with expressions, you'll need to use many different mathematical properties and operations, including addition/subtraction, multiplication/division, exponents, roots, distribution, and the order of operations.

Evaluating Algebraic Expressions

To evaluate an algebraic expression, simply plug the given value(s) in for the appropriate variable(s) in the expression.

> **Example**
>
> Evaluate $2x + 6y - 3z$ if $x = 2$, $y = 4$, and $z = -3$.
>
> Plug in each number for the correct variable and simplify:
>
> $2x + 6y - 3z = 2(2) + 6(4) - 3(-3) = 4 + 24 + 9 = \textbf{37}$

Adding and Subtracting Expressions

Only LIKE TERMS, which have the exact same variable(s), can be added or subtracted. CONSTANTS are numbers without variables attached, and those can be added and subtracted together as well. When simplifying an expression, like terms should be added or subtracted so that no individual group of variables occurs in more than one term. For example, the expression $5x + 6xy$ is in its simplest form, while $5x + 6xy - 11xy$ is not because the term xy appears more than once.

> **Example**
>
> Simplify the expression $5xy + 7y + 2yz + 11xy - 5yz$
>
> Start by grouping together like terms:
>
> $(5xy + 11xy) + (2yz - 5yz) + 7y$
>
> Now you can add together each set of like terms:
>
> $\textbf{16xy + 7y - 3yz}$

Multiplying and Dividing Expressions

To multiply a single term by another, simply multiply the coefficients and then multiply the variables. Remember that when multiplying variables with exponents, those exponents are added together. For example, $(x^5 y)(x^3 y^4) = x^8 y^5$.

When multiplying a term by a set of terms inside parentheses, you need to DISTRIBUTE to each term inside the parentheses as shown below:

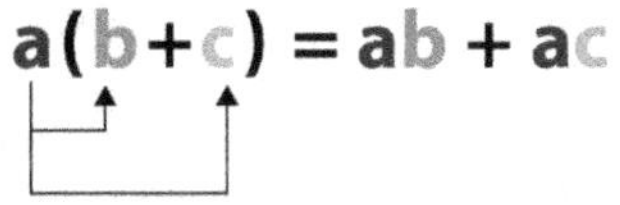

$$a(b + c) = ab + ac$$

Figure 1.2. Distribution

When variables occur in both the numerator and denominator of a fraction, they cancel each other out. So, a fraction with variables in its simplest form will not have the same variable on the top and bottom.

Examples

1. Simplify the expression $(3x^4y^2z)(2y^4z^5)$.

Multiply the coefficients and variables together:

$3 \times 2 = 6$

$y^2 \times y^4 = y^6$

$z \times z^5 = z^6$

Now put all the terms back together:

$6x^4y^6z^6$

2. Simplify the expression: $(2y^2)(y^3 + 2xy^2z + 4z)$

Multiply each term inside the parentheses by the term $2y^2$:

$(2y^2)(y^3 + 2xy^2z + 4z) =$

$(2y^2 \times y^3) + (2y^2 \times 2xy^2z) \times (2y^2 \times 4z) =$

$2y^5 + 4xy^4z + 8y^2z$

3. Simplify the expression: $(5x + 2)(3x + 3)$

Use the acronym FOIL—first, outer, inner, last—to multiply the terms:

first: $5x \times 3x = 15x^2$

outer: $5x \times 3 = 15x$

inner: $2 \times 3x = 6x$

last: $2 \times 3 = 6$

Now combine like terms:

$15x^2 + 21x + 6$

4. Simplify the expression: $\dfrac{2x^4y^3z}{8x^2z^2}$

Simplify by looking at each variable and checking for those that appear in the numerator and denominator:

$\dfrac{2}{8} = \dfrac{1}{4}$

$\dfrac{x^4}{x^2} = \dfrac{x^2}{1}$

$\dfrac{z}{z^2} = \dfrac{1}{z}$

$\dfrac{2x^4y^3z}{8x^2z^2} = \dfrac{x^2y^3}{4z}$

⚠️ —————————————

When multiplying terms, add the exponents. When dividing, subtract the exponents.

Factoring Expressions

FACTORING is splitting one expression into the multiplication of two expressions. It requires finding the HIGHEST COMMON FACTOR and dividing terms by that number. For example, in the expression $15x + 10$, the highest common factor is 5 because both terms are divisible by 5: $\dfrac{15x}{5} = 3x$ and $\dfrac{10}{5} = 2$. When you factor the expression you get $5(3x + 2)$.

Sometimes it is difficult to find the highest common factor. In these cases, consider whether the expression fits a polynomial identity. A **POLYNOMIAL** is an expression with more than one term. If you can recognize the common polynomials listed below, you can easily factor the expression.

$$a^2 - b^2 = (a + b)(a - b)$$

$$a^2 + 2ab + b^2 = (a + b)(a + b) = (a + b)^2$$

$$a^2 - 2ab + b^2 = (a - b)(a - b) = (a - b)^2$$

Examples

1. Factor the expression $27x^2 - 9x$

   First, find the highest common factor. Both terms are divisible by 9:

   $\frac{27x^2}{9} = 3x^2$ and $\frac{9x}{9} = x$

   Now the expression is $9(3x^2 - x)$ – but wait, you're not done! Both terms can be divided by x:

   $\frac{3x^2}{x} = 3x$ and $\frac{x}{x} = 1$.

   The final factored expression is **$9x(3x - 1)$**.

2. Factor the expression $25x^2 - 16$

   Since there is no obvious factor by which you can divide terms, you should consider whether this expression fits one of your polynomial identities.

   This expression is a difference of squares $a^2 - b^2$, where $a^2 = 25x^2$ and $b^2 = 16$.

   Recall that $a^2 - b^2 = (a + b)(a - b)$. Now solve for a and b:

   $a = \sqrt{25x^2} = 5x$

   $b = \sqrt{16} = 4$

   $(a + b)(a - b) = $ **$(5x + 4)(5x - 4)$**

   You can check your work by using the FOIL acronym to expand your answer back to the original expression:

   first: $5x \times 5x = 25x^2$

   outer: $5x \times -4 = -20x$

   inner: $4 \times 5x = 20x$

   last: $4 \times -4 = -16$

   $25x^2 - 20x + 20x - 16 = 25x^2 - 16$

3. Factor the expression $100x^2 + 60x + 9$

   This is another polynomial identity, $a^2 + 2ab + b^2$. (The more you practice these problems, the faster you will recognize polynomial identities.)

   $a^2 = 100x^2$, $2ab = 60x$, and $b^2 = 9$

   Recall that $a^2 + 2ab + b^2 = (a + b)^2$. Now solve for a and b:

   $a = \sqrt{100x^2} = 10x$

   $b = \sqrt{9} = 3$

(Double check your work by confirming that $2ab = 2 \times 10x \times 3 = 60x$)

$(a + b)^2 = (10x + 3)^2$

Linear Equations

An **EQUATION** is a statement saying that two expressions are equal to each other. They always include an equal sign (e.g., $3x + 2xy = 17$). A **LINEAR EQUATION** has only two variables; on a graph, linear equations form a straight line.

Solving Linear Equations

To solve an equation, you need to manipulate the terms on each side to isolate the variable, meaning if you want to find x, you have to get the x alone on one side of the equal sign. To do this, you'll need to use many of the tools discussed above: you might need to distribute, divide, add or subtract like terms, or find common denominators.

Think of each side of the equation as the two sides of a see-saw. As long as the two people on each end weigh the same amount (no matter what it is) the see-saw will be balanced: if you have a 120 pound person on each end, the see-saw is balanced. Giving each of them a 10 pound rock to hold changes the weight on each end, but the see-saw itself stays balanced. Equations work the same way: you can add, subtract, multiply, or divide whatever you want as long as you do the same thing to both sides.

Most equations you'll see on the PERT can be solved using the same basic steps:

1. distribute to get rid of parentheses
2. use LCD to get rid of fractions
3. add/subtract like terms on either side
4. add/subtract so that constants appear on only one side of the equation
5. multiply/divide to isolate the variable

Examples

1. Solve for x: $25x + 12 = 62$

This equation has no parentheses, fractions, or like terms on the same side, so you can start by subtracting 12 from both sides of the equation:

$25x + 12 = 62$

$(25x + 12) - 12 = 62 - 12$

$25x = 50$

Now, divide by 25 to isolate the variable:

$\frac{25x}{25} = \frac{50}{25}$

$x = 2$

2. Solve the following equation for x: $2x - 4(2x + 3) = 24$

Start by distributing to get rid of the parentheses (don't forget to distribute the negative):

$2x - 4(2x + 3) = 24$

$2x - 8x - 12 = 24$

There are no fractions, so now you can join like terms:

$2x - 8x - 12 = 24$

$-6x - 12 = 24$

Now add 12 to both sides and divide by -6.

$-6x - 12 = 24$

$(-6x - 12) + 12 = 24 + 12$

$-6x = 36$

$\frac{-6x}{-6} = \frac{36}{-6}$

$\boldsymbol{x = -6}$

3. Solve the following equation for x: $\frac{x}{3} + \frac{1}{2} = \frac{x}{6} - \frac{5}{12}$

Start by multiplying by the least common denominator to get rid of the fractions:

$\frac{x}{3} + \frac{1}{2} = \frac{x}{6} - \frac{5}{12}$

$\frac{12x}{3} + \frac{1}{2} = \frac{12x}{6} - \frac{5}{12}$

$4x + 6 = 2x - 5$

Now you can isolate the x:

$(4x + 6) - 6 = (2x - 5) - 6 \rightarrow$

$4x = 2x - 11 \rightarrow$

$(4x) - 2x = (2x - 11) - 2x \rightarrow$

$2x = -11$

$\boldsymbol{x = -\frac{11}{2}}$

4. Find the value of x: $2(x + y) - 7x = 14x + 3$

This equation looks more difficult because it has 2 variables, but you can use the same steps to solve for x. First, distribute to get rid of the parentheses and combine like terms:

$2(x + y) - 7x = 14x + 3 \rightarrow$

$2x + 2y - 7x = 14x + 3 \rightarrow$

$-5x + 2y = 14x + 3$

Now you can move the x terms to one side and everything else to the other, and then divide to isolate x:

$-5x + 2y = 14x + 3 \rightarrow$

$-19x = -2y + 3 \rightarrow$

$\boldsymbol{x = \frac{2y - 3}{19}}$

Graphing Linear Equations

Linear equations can be plotted as straight lines on a coordinate plane. The x-AXIS is always the horizontal axis and the Y-AXIS is always the vertical axis. The x-axis is positive to the right of the y-axis and negative to the left. The y-axis is positive above the x-axis and negative below. To describe the location of any point on the graph, write the coordinates in the form (x, y). The origin, the point where the x- and y-axes cross, is $(0, 0)$.

The y-intercept is the y coordinate where the line crosses the y-axis. The slope is a measure of how steep the line is. **SLOPE** is calculated by dividing the change along the y-axis by the change along the x-axis between any two points on the line.

Linear equations are easiest to graph when they are written in **POINT-SLOPE FORM**: $y = mx + b$. The constant m represents slope and the constant b represents the y-intercept. If you know two points along the line (x_1, y_1) and (x_2, y_2), you can calculate slope using the following equation: $m = \frac{y_2 - y_1}{x_2 - x_1}$. If you know the slope and one other point along the line, you can calculate the y-intercept by plugging the number 0 in for x_2 and solving for y_2.

When graphing a linear equation, first plot the y-intercept. Next, plug in values for x to solve for y and plot additional points. Connect the points with a straight line.

Examples

1. Find the slope of the line: $\frac{3y}{2} + 3 = x$

   Slope is easiest to find when the equation is in point-slope form ($y = mx + b$). Rearrange the equation to isolate y:

   $\frac{3y}{2} + 3 = x$

   $3y + 6 = 2x$

   $y + 2 = \frac{2x}{3}$

   $y = \frac{2x}{3} - 2$

   Finally, identify the term m to find the slope of the line:

   $m = \frac{2}{3}$

2. Plot the linear equation $2y - 4x = 6$

   First, rearrange the linear equation to point-slope form ($y = mx + b$):

   $2y - 4x = 6$

   $y = 2x + 3$

   Next, identify the y-intercept (b) and the slope (m):

   $b = 3, m = 2$

   Now, plot the y-intercept $(0, b) =$ **(0, 3)**:

   Next, plug in values for x and solve for y:

   $y = 2(1) + 3 = 5 \rightarrow$ **(1,5)**

$y = 2(-1) + 3 = 1 \rightarrow \textbf{(–1,1)}$

Plot these points on the graph, and connect the points with a straight line:

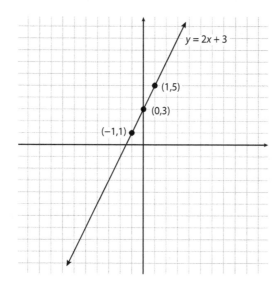

Systems of Equations

A system of equations is a group of related questions sharing the same variable. The problems you see on the PERT will most likely involve two equations that each have two variables, although you may also solve sets of equations with any number of variables as long as there are a corresponding number of equations (e.g., to solve a system with four variables, you need four equations).

There are two main methods used to solve systems of equations. In **SUBSTITUTION**, solve one equation for a single variable, then substitute the solution for that variable into the second equation to solve for the other variable. Or, you can use **ELIMINATION** by adding equations together to cancel variables and solve for one of them.

Examples

1. Solve the following system of equations: $3y - 4 + x = 0$
   and
   $5x + 6y = 11$

   To solve this system using substitution, first solve one equation for a single variable:

   $3y - 4 + x = 0$

   $3y + x = 4$

   $x = 4 - 3y$

   Next, substitute the expression to the right of the equal sign for x in the second equation:

   $5x + 6y = 11$

   $5(4 - 3y) + 6y = 11$

   $20 - 15y + 6y = 11$

   $20 - 9y = 11$

$-9y = -9$

$y = 1$

Finally, plug the value for y back into the first equation to find the value of x:

$3y - 4 + x = 0$

$3(1) - 4 + x = 0$

$-1 + x = 0$

$x = 1$

The solution is **$x = 1$** and **$y = 1$**, or the point **(1, 1)**.

2. Solve the system $2x + 4y = 8$ and $4x + 2y = 10$

To solve this system using elimination, start by manipulating one equation so that a variable (in this case x) will cancel when the equations are added together:

$2x + 4y = 8$

$-2(2x + 4y = 8)$

$-4x - 8y = -16$

Now you can add the two equations together, and the x variable will drop out:

$-4x - 8y = -16$

$\underline{4x + 2y = 10}$

$-6y = -6$

$y = 1$

Lastly, plug the y value into one of the equations to find the value of x:

$2x + 4y = 8$

$2x + 4(1) = 8$

$2x + 4 = 8$

$2x = 4$

$x = 2$

The solution is **$x = 2$** and **$y = 1$**, or the point **(2, 1)**.

Building Equations

Word problems describe a situation or a problem without explicitly providing an equation to solve. It is up to you to build an algebraic equation to solve the problem. You must translate the words into mathematical operations. Represent the quantity you do not know with a variable. If there is more than one unknown, you will likely have to write more than one equation, then solve the system of equations by substituting expressions. Make sure you keep your variables straight!

Examples

1. David, Jesse and Mark shoveled snow during their snow day and made a total of $100. They agreed to split it based on how much each person worked. David will take $10 more than Jesse, who will take $15 more than Mark.

How much money will David get?

Start by building an equation. David's amount will be d, Jesse's amount will be j, and Mark's amount will be m. All three must add up to $100:

$$d + j + m = 100$$

It may seem like there are three unknowns in this situation, but you can express j and m in terms of d:

Jesse gets $10 less than David, so $j = d - 10$. Mark gets $15 less than Jesse, so $m = j - 15$.

Substitute the previous expression for j to solve for m in terms of d:

$$m = (d - 10) - 15 = d - 25$$

Now back to our original equation, substituting for j and m:

$$d + (d - 10) + (d - 25) = 100$$

$$3d - 35 = 100$$

$$3d = 135$$

$$d = 45$$

David will get **$45**.

2. The sum of three consecutive numbers is 54. What is the middle number?

Start by building an equation. One of the numbers in question will be x. The three numbers are consecutive, so if x is the smallest number then the other two numbers must be $(x + 1)$ and $(x + 2)$. You know that the sum of the three numbers is 54:

$$x + (x + 1) + (x + 2) = 54$$

Now solve for the equation to find x:

$$3x + 3 = 54$$

$$3x = 51$$

$$x = 17$$

The question asks about the middle number $(x + 1)$, so the answer is **18**.

Notice that you could have picked any number to be x. If you picked the middle number as x, your equation would be: $(x - 1) + x + (x + 1) = 54$. Solve for x to get 18.

3. There are 42 people on the varsity football team. This is 8 more than half the number of people on the swim team. There are 6 fewer boys on the swim team than girls. How many girls are on the swim team?

This word problem might seem complicated at first, but as long as you keep your variables straight and translate the words into mathematical operations you can easily build an equation. The quantity you want to solve is the number of girls on the swim team, so this will be x.

The number of boys on the swim team will be y. There are 6 fewer boys than girls so $y = x - 6$.

The total number of boys and girls on the swim team is $x + y$.

42 is 8 more than half this number, so $42 = 8 + (x + y) \div 2$

Now substitute for y to solve for x:

$42 = 8 + (x + x - 6) \div 2$

$34 = (2x - 6) \div 2$

$68 = 2x - 6$

$74 = 2x$

$x = 37$

There are **37 girls** on the swim team.

LINEAR INEQUALITIES

INEQUALITIES look like equations, except that instead of having an equal sign, they have one of the following symbols:

> greater than: the expression left of the symbol is larger than the expression on the right

< less than: the expression left of the symbol is smaller than the expression on the right

≥ greater than or equal to: the expression left of the symbol is larger than or equal to the expression on the right

≤ less than or equal to: the expression left of the symbol is less than or equal to the expression on the right

Solving Linear Inequalities

Inequalities are solved like linear and algebraic equations. The only difference is that the symbol must be reversed when both sides of the equation are multiplied by a negative number.

See *Solving Linear Equations* for step-by-step instructions on solving basic equations.

Example

Solve for x: $-7x + 2 < 6 - 5x$

Collect like terms on each side as you would for a regular equation:

$-7x + 2 < 6 - 5x \rightarrow$

$-2x < 4$

When you divide by a negative number, the direction of the sign switches:

$-2x < 4 \rightarrow$

$x > -2$

Graphing Linear Inequalities

Graphing a linear inequality is just like graphing a linear equation, except that you shade the area on one side of the line. To graph a linear inequality, first rearrange the inequality expression into $y =$

mx + *b* form. Then treat the inequality symbol like an equal sign and plot the line. If the inequality symbol is < or >, make a broken line; for ≤ or ≥, make a solid line. Finally, shade the correct side of the graph:

For *y* < *mx* + *b* or *y* ≤ *mx* + *b*, shade the side below the line.

For *y* > *mx* + *b* or *y* ≥ *mx* + *b*, shade the side above the line.

Examples

Plot the inequality $3x \geq 4 - y$

> To rearrange the inequality into $y = mx + b$ form, first subtract 4 from both sides:
>
> $3x - 4 \geq -y$
>
> Next divide both sides by −1 to get positive *y*; remember to switch the direction of the inequality symbol:
>
> $-3x + 4 \leq y$
>
> Now plot the line $y = -3x + 4$, making a solid line:
>
> Finally, shade the side above the line:

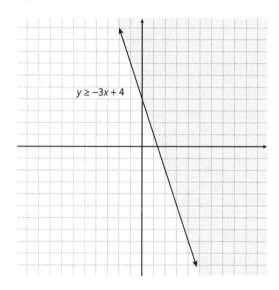

$y \geq -3x + 4$

QUADRATIC EQUATIONS

A quadratic equation is any equation in the form $ax^2 + bx + c = 0$. In quadratic equations, *x* is the variable and *a*, *b*, and *c* are all known numbers. *a* cannot be 0.

Solving Quadratic Equations

There is more than one way to solve a quadratic equation. One way is by **FACTORING**. By rearranging the expression $ax\_^2 + bx + c$ into one factor multiplied by another factor, you can easily solve for the **ROOTS**, the values of *x* for which the quadratic expression equals 0. Another way to solve a quadratic equation is by using **THE QUADRATIC FORMULA**: $x = \frac{-b \pm \sqrt{b^2 - 4ac}}{2a}$. The expression $b^2 - 4ac$ is called the **DISCRIMINANT**; when it is positive you will get two real numbers for *x*, when it is negative you will get one real number and one imaginary number for x, and when it is zero you will get one real number for x.

Examples

1. Factor the quadratic equation $-2x^2 = 14x$ and find the roots.

Not every quadratic equation you see will be presented in the standard form. Rearrange terms to set one side equal to 0:

$2x^2 + 14x = 0$

Note that $a = 2$, $b = 14$, and $c = 0$ because there is no third term.

Now divide the expression on the left by the common factor:

$(2x)(x + 7) = 0$

To find the roots, set each of the factors equal to 0:

$2x = 0 \rightarrow \boldsymbol{x = 0}$

$x + 7 = 0 \rightarrow \boldsymbol{x = -7}$

2. Use the quadratic formula to solve for x: $3x^2 = 7x - 2$

First rearrange the equation to set one side equal to 0:

$3x^2 - 7x + 2 = 0$

Next identify the terms a, b, and c:

$a = 3$, $b = -7$, $c = 2$

Now plug those terms into the quadratic formula:

$x = \dfrac{-b \pm \sqrt{b^2 - 4ac}}{2a}$

$x = \dfrac{7 \pm \sqrt{(-7)^2 - 4(3)(2)}}{2(3)}$

$x = \dfrac{7 \pm \sqrt{25}}{6}$

$x = \dfrac{7 \pm 5}{6}$

Since the determinant is positive, you can expect two real numbers for x. Solve for the two possible answers:

$x = \dfrac{7 + 5}{6} \rightarrow \boldsymbol{x = 2}$

$x = \dfrac{7 - 5}{6} \rightarrow \boldsymbol{x = \dfrac{1}{3}}$

Graphing Quadratic Equations

Graphing a quadratic equation forms a PARABOLA. A parabola is a symmetrical, horseshoe-shaped curve; a vertical axis passes through its vertex. Each term in the equation $ax^2 + bx + c = 0$ affects the shape of the parabola. A bigger value for a makes the curve narrower, while a smaller value makes the curve wider. A negative value for a flips the parabola upside down. The AXIS OF SYMMETRY is the vertical line $x = \dfrac{-b}{2a}$. To find the y-coordinate for the VERTEX, plug this value for x into the expression $ax^2 + bx + c$. The easiest way to graph a quadratic equation is to find the axis of symmetry, solve for the vertex, and then create a table of points by plugging in other numbers for x and solving for y. Plot these points and trace the parabola.

Examples

Graph the equation $x^2 + 4x + 1 = 0$

First, find the axis of symmetry. The equation for the line of symmetry is $x = \frac{-b}{2a}$.

$x = \frac{-4}{2(1)} = -2$

Next, plug in −2 for x to find the y coordinate of the vertex:

$y = (-2)^2 + 4(-2) + 1 = -3$

The vertex is (−2, −3)

Now, make a table of points on either side of the vertex by plugging in numbers for x and solving for y:

x	$y = x^2 + 4x + 1$	(x, y)
−3	$y = (-3)^2 + 4(-3) + 1 = -2$	(−3, −2)
−1	$y = (-1)^2 + 4(-1) + 1 = -2$	(−1, −2)
−4	$y = (-4)^2 + 4(-4) + 1 = 1$	(−4, 1)
0	$y = (0)^2 + 4(0) + 1 = 1$	(0, 1)

Finally, draw the axis of symmetry, plot the vertex and your table of points, and trace the parabola:

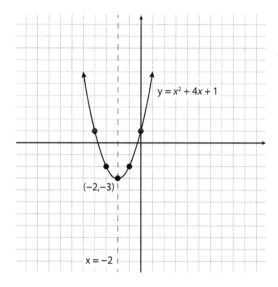

FUNCTIONS

FUNCTIONS describe how an input relates to an output. Linear equations, sine and cosine are examples of functions. In a function, there must be one and only one output for each input. $\sqrt{x}$ is not a function because there are two outputs for any one input: $\sqrt{4} = 2, -2$.

→
CONTINUE

Describing Functions

Functions are often written in $f(x)$ form: $f(x) = x^2$ means that for input x the output is x^2. In relating functions to linear equations, you can think of $f(x)$ as equivalent to y. The DOMAIN of a function is all the possible inputs of that function. The RANGE of a function includes the outputs of the inputs. For example, for the function $f(x) = x^2$, if the domain includes all positive and negative integers the range will include 0 and only positive integers. When you graph a function, the domain is plotted on the x-axis and the range is plotted on the y-axis.

Examples

1. Given $f(x) = 2x - 10$, find $f(9)$.

   Plug in 9 for x:

   $f(9) = 2(9) - 10$

   $f(9) = 8$

2. Given $f(x) = \frac{4}{x}$ with a domain of all positive integers except zero, and $g(x) = \frac{4}{x}$ with a domain of all positive and negative integers except zero, which function has a range that includes the number -2?

   The function $f(x)$ has a range of only positive numbers, since x cannot be negative. The function $g(x)$ has a range of positive and negative numbers, since x can be either positive or negative. **The number -2, therefore, must be in the range for $g(x)$ but not for $f(x)$.**

Exponential Functions

An EXPONENTIAL FUNCTION is in the form $f(x) = a^x$, where $a > 0$. When $a > 1$, $f(x)$ approaches infinity as x increases and zero as x decreases. When $0 < a < 1$, $f(x)$ approaches zero as x increases and infinity as x increases. When $a = 1$, $f(x) = 1$. The graph of an exponential function where $a \neq 1$ will have a horizontal asymptote along the x-axis; the graph will never cross below the x-axis. The graph of an exponential function where $a = 1$ will be a horizontal line at $y = 1$. All graphs of exponential functions include the points $(0, 1)$ and $(1, a)$.

Examples

1. Graph the function $f(x) = 3^x$.

   First, estimate the shape and direction of the graph based on the value of a. Since $a > 1$, you know that $f(x)$ will approach infinity as x increases and there will be a horizontal asymptote along the negative x-axis.

   Next, plot the points $(0, 1)$ and $(1, a)$.

   Finally, plug in one or two more values for x, plot those points and trace the graph:

   $f(2) = 3^2 = 9 \rightarrow (2, 9)$

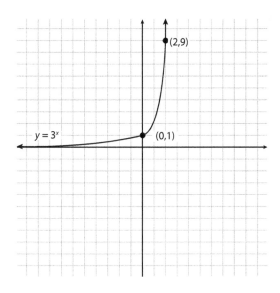

2. Given $f(x) = 2^x$, solve for x when $f(x) = 64$.

$64 = 2^x$

The inverse of an exponent is a log. Take the log of both sides to solve for x:

$\log_2 64 = x$

$\boldsymbol{x = 6}$

Logarithmic Functions

A **LOGARITHMIC FUNCTION** is the inverse of an exponential function. Remember the definition of a log: if $\log_a x = b$, then $a^b = x$. Logarithmic functions are written in the form $f(x) = \log_a x$, where a is any number greater than 0, except for 1. If a is not shown, it is assumed that $a = 10$. The function $\ln x$ is called a **NATURAL LOG**, equal to $\log_e x$. When $0 < a < 1$, $f(x)$ approaches infinity as x approaches zero and negative infinity as x increases. When $a > 1$, $f(x)$ approaches negative infinity as x approaches zero and infinity as x increases. In either case, the graph of a logarithmic function has a vertical asymptote along the y-axis; the graph will never cross to the left of the y-axis. All graphs of logarithmic functions include the points $(1, 0)$ and $(a, 1)$.

Examples

1. Graph the function $f(x) = \log_4 x$.

First, estimate the shape and direction of the graph based on the value of a. Since $a > 1$, you know that $f(x)$ will approach infinity as x increases and there will be a vertical asymptote along the negative y-axis.

Next, plot the points $(1, 0)$ and $(a, 1)$.

Finally, it is easier to plug in a value for $f(x)$ and solve for x rather than attempting to solve for $f(x)$. Plug in one or two values for $f(x)$, plot those points and trace the graph:

$2 = \log_4 x$

$4^2 = x$

$16 = x \rightarrow (16, 2)$

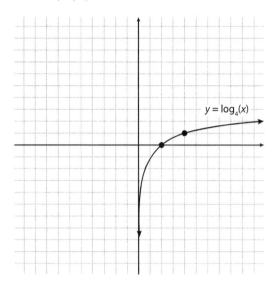

$y = \log_4(x)$

2. Given $f(x) = \log_{\frac{1}{3}} x$, solve for $f(81)$.

Rewrite the function in exponent form:

$x = \frac{1}{3}^{f(x)}$

$81 = \frac{1}{3}^{f(x)}$

The question is asking: to what power must you raise $\frac{1}{3}$ to get 81?

Recognize that $3^4 = 81$, so $\frac{1}{3}^4 = \frac{1}{81}$

Switch the sign of the exponent to flip the numerator and denominator:

$\frac{1}{3}^{-4} = \frac{81}{1}$

$f(81) = -4$

Arithmetic and Geometric Sequences

SEQUENCES are patterns of numbers. In most questions about sequences you must determine the pattern. In an ARITHMETIC SEQUENCE, add or subtract the same number between terms. In a GEOMETRIC SEQUENCE, multiply or divide by the same number between terms. For example, 2, 6, 10, 14, 18 and 11, 4, −3, −10, −17 are arithmetic sequences because you add 4 to each term in the first example and you subtract 7 from each term in the second example. The sequence 5, 15, 45, 135 is a geometric sequence because you multiply each term by 3. In arithmetic sequences, the number by which you add or subtract is called the COMMON DIFFERENCE. In geometric sequences, the number by which you multiply or divide is called the COMMON RATIO.

In an arithmetic sequence, the nth term (a_n) can be found by calculating $a_n = a_1 + (n - 1)d$, where d is the common difference and a_1 is the first term in the sequence. In a geometric sequence, $a_n = a_1(r^n)$, where r is the common ratio.

Examples

1. Find the common difference and the next term of the following sequence: 5, −1, −7, −13

   Find the difference between two terms that are next to each other:

   $5 - (-1) = -6$

   The common difference is −6. (It must be negative to show the difference is subtracted, not added.)

   Now subtract 7 from the last term to find the next term:

   $-13 - 6 = -19$

   The next term is −19.

2. Find the 12th term of the following sequence: 2, 6, 18, 54

   First, decide whether this is an arithmetic or geometric sequence. Since the numbers are getting farther and farther apart, you know this must be a geometric sequence.

   Divide one term by the term before it to find the common ratio:

   $18 \div 6 = 3$

   Next, plug in the common ratio and the first term to the equation $a_n = a_1(r^n)$:

   $a_{12} = 2(3^{12})$

   $a_{12} = 1,062,882$

   Notice that it would have taken a very long time to multiply each term by 3 until you got the 12th term—this is where that equation comes in handy!

3. The fourth term of a sequence is 9. The common difference is 11. What is the 10th term?

   To answer this question, you can simply add $9 + 11 = 20$ to get the 5th term, $20 + 11 = 31$ to get the 6th term, and so on until you get the 10th term. Or you can plug the information you know into your equation $a_n = a_1 + (n - 1)d$. In this case, you do not know the first term. If you use the fourth term instead, you must replace $(n - 1)$ with $(n - 4)$:

   $a_{10} = 9 + (10 - 4)11$

   $a_{10} = 75$

ABSOLUTE VALUE

The **ABSOLUTE VALUE** of a number (represented by the symbol $|x|$) is its distance from zero, not its value. For example, $|3| = 3$, and $|-3| = 3$ because both 3 and −3 are three units from zero. The absolute value of a number is always positive.

Equations with absolute values will have two answers, so you need to set up two equations. The first is simply the equation with the absolute value symbol removed. For the second equation, isolate the absolute value on one side of the equation and multiply the other side of the equation by -1.

Examples

1. Solve for x: $|2x - 3| = x + 1$

   Set up the first equation by removing the absolute value symbol then solve for x:

   $|2x - 3| = x + 1$

   $2x - 3 = x + 1$

   $x = 4$

   For the second equation, remove the absolute value and multiply by -1:

   $|2x - 3| = x + 1 \rightarrow$

   $2x - 3 = -(x + 1) \rightarrow$

   $2x - 3 = -x - 1 \rightarrow$

   $3x = 2$

   $x = \frac{2}{3}$

   Both answers are correct, so the complete answer is **$x = 4$ or $\frac{2}{3}$.**

2. Solve for y: $2|y + 4| = 10$

   Set up the first equation:

   $2(y + 4) = 10$

   $y + 4 = 5$

   $y = 1$

   Set up the second equation. Remember to isolate the absolute value before multiplying by -1:

   $2|y + 4| = 10 \rightarrow$

   $|y + 4| = 5 \rightarrow$

   $y + 4 = -5$

   $y = -9$

   $y = 1$ or -9

SOLVING WORD PROBLEMS

Any of the math concepts discussed here can be turned into a word problem, and you'll likely see word problems in various forms throughout the test. (In fact, you may have noticed that several examples in the ratio and proportion sections were word problems.)

Be sure to read the entire problem before beginning to solve it: a common mistake is to provide an answer to a question that wasn't actually asked. Also, remember that not all of the information provided in a problem is necessarily needed to solve it.

When working multiple-choice word problems like those on the PERT, it's important to check your work. Many of the incorrect answer choices will be those resulting from common mistakes. So even if a solution you calculated is listed as an answer choice, that doesn't necessarily mean you've done the problem correctly—you have to check your own answer to be sure.

General Steps for Word Problem Solving

Step 1: Read the entire problem and determine what the question is asking.

Step 2: List all of the given data and define the variables.

Step 3: Determine the formula(s) needed or set up equations from the information in the problem.

Step 4: Solve.

Step 5: Check your answer. (Is the amount too large or small? Are the answers in the correct unit of measure?)

Basic Word Problems

A word problem in algebra is just an equation or a set of equations described using words. Your task when solving these problems is to turn the "story" of the problem into mathematical equations.

Examples

1. A store owner bought a case of 75 backpacks for $476.00. He sold 17 of the backpacks in his store for $18 each, and the rest were sold to a school for $15 each. What was the store owner's profit?

   Start by listing all the data and defining the variable:

   total number of backpacks = 75

   cost of backpacks = $476.00

   backpacks sold in store at price of $18 = 17

   backpacks sold to school at a price of $15 = 75 − 17 = 58

   total profit = x

   Now set up an equation:

   total profit = income − cost

   $x = [(17 \times 18) + (58 \times 15)] - 476$

   $x = 1176 - 476 = 700$

   The store owner made a profit of **$700**.

2. Thirty students in Mr. Joyce's room are working on projects over 2 days. The first day, he gave them $\frac{3}{5}$ hour to work. On the second day, he gave them $\frac{1}{2}$ as much time as the first day. How much time did each student have to work on the project?

Coverting units can often help you avoid operations with fractions when dealing with time.

Start by listing all the data and defining your variables. Note that the number of students, while given in the problem, is not needed to find the answer:

time on 1st day = $\frac{3}{5}$ hr. = 36 min.

time on 2nd day = $\frac{1}{2}(36)$ = 18 min.

total time = x

Now set up the equation and solve:

total time = time on 1st day + time on 2nd day

$x = 36 + 18 = 54$

The students had **54 minutes** to work on the projects.

Distance Word Problems

Distance word problems involve something traveling at a constant or average speed. Whenever you read a problem that involves *how fast*, *how far*, or *for how long*, you should think of the distance equation $d = rt$, where d stands for distance, r for rate (speed), and t for time.

These problems can be solved by setting up a grid with d, r, and t along the top and each moving object on the left. When setting up the grid, make sure the units are consistent. For example, if the distance is in meters and the time is in seconds, the rate should be meters per second.

Examples

1. Will drove from his home to the airport at an average speed of 30 mph. He then boarded a helicopter and flew to the hospital at an average speed of 60 mph. The entire distance was 150 miles, and the trip took 3 hours. Find the distance from the airport to the hospital.

   The first step is to set up a table and fill in a value for each variable:

	d	r	t
driving	d	30	t
flying	$150 - d$	60	$3 - t$

   You can now set up equations for driving and flying. The first row gives the equation $d = 30t$ and the second row gives the equation $150 - d = 60(3 - t)$.

   Next, solve this system of equations. Start by substituting for d in the second equation:

   $d = 30t$

   $150 - d = 60(30 - t) \rightarrow 150 - 30t = 60(30 - t)$

   Now solve for t:

   $150 - 30t = 180 - 60t$

   $-30 = -30t$

   $1 = t$

Although you've solved for t, you're not done yet. Notice that the problem asks for distance. So, you need to solve for d: what the problem asked for. It does not ask for time, but you need to calculate it to solve the problem.

Driving: $30t = 30$ miles

Flying: $150 - d = 120$ miles

The distance from the airport to the hospital is **120 miles**.

2. Two riders on horseback start at the same time from opposite ends of a field that is 45 miles long. One horse is moving at 14 mph and the second horse is moving at 16 mph. How long after they begin will they meet?

First, set up the table. The variable for time will be the same for each, because they will have been on the field for the same amount of time when they meet:

	d	r	t
horse #1	d	14	t
horse #2	$45 - d$	16	t

Next set up two equations:

Horse #1: $d = 14t$

Horse #2: $45 - d = 16t$

Now substitute and solve:

$d = 14t$

$45 - d = 16t \rightarrow 45 - 14t = 16t$

$45 = 30t$

$t = 1.5$

They will meet **1.5 hr.** after they begin.

Work Problems

WORK PROBLEMS involve situations where several people or machines are doing work at different rates. Your task is usually to figure out how long it will take these people or machines to complete a task while working together. The trick to doing work problems is to figure out how much of the project each person or machine completes in the same unit of time. For example, you might calculate how much of a wall a person can paint in 1 hour, or how many boxes an assembly line can pack in 1 minute.

The next step is to set up an equation to solve for the total time. This equation is usually similar to the equation for distance, but here *work = rate × time*.

Examples

1. Bridget can clean an entire house in 12 hours while her brother Tom takes 8 hours. How long would it take for Bridget and Tom to clean 2 houses together?

The PERT will give you most of the formulas you need to work problems, but they won't give you the formulas for percent change or work problems.

See *Adding and Subtracting Fractions* for step-by-step instruction on operations with fractions.

Start by figuring out how much of a house each sibling can clean on his or her own. Bridget can clean the house in 12 hours, so she can clean $\frac{1}{12}$ of the house in an hour. Using the same logic, Tom can clean $\frac{1}{8}$ of a house in an hour.

By adding these values together, you get the fraction of the house they can clean together in an hour :

$$\frac{1}{12} + \frac{1}{8} = \frac{5}{24}$$

They can do $\frac{5}{24}$ of the job per hour.

Now set up variables and an equation to solve:

t = time spent cleaning (in hours)

h = number of houses cleaned = 2

work = rate × time

$h = \frac{5}{24}t \rightarrow$

$2 = \frac{5}{24}t \rightarrow$

$t = \frac{48}{5} = \mathbf{9\frac{3}{5}}$ **hr.**

2. Farmer Dan needs to water his cornfield. One hose can water a field 1.25 times faster than a second hose. When both hoses are running, they water the field together in 5 hours. How long would it take to water the field if only the slower hose is used?

   In this problem you don't know the exact time, but you can still find the hourly rate as a variable:

   The second hose completes the job in f hours, so it waters $\frac{1}{f}$ field per hour. The faster hose waters the field in 1.25f, so it waters the field in $\frac{1}{1.25f}$ hours. Together, they take 5 hours to water the field, so they water $\frac{1}{5}$ of the field per hour.

   Now you can set up the equations and solve:

   $\frac{1}{f} + \frac{1}{1.25f} = \frac{1}{5} \rightarrow$

   $1.25f \left(\frac{1}{f} + \frac{1}{1.25f} \right) = 1.25f \left(\frac{1}{5} \right) \rightarrow$

   $1.25 + 1 = 0.25f$

   $2.25 = 0.25f$

   $f = 9$

   The fast hose takes 9 hours to water the field. The slow hose takes 1.25(9) = **11.25 hours**.

3. Martha takes 2 hours to pick 500 apples, and George takes 3 hours to pick 450 apples. How long will they take, working together, to pick 1000 apples?

   Calculate how many apples each person can pick per hour:

   Martha: $\frac{500 \text{ apples}}{2 \text{ hrs}} = \frac{250 \text{ apples}}{\text{hr}}$

   George: $\frac{450 \text{ apples}}{3 \text{ hrs}} = \frac{150 \text{ apples}}{\text{hr}}$

   Together: $\frac{(250 + 150) \text{apples}}{\text{hr}} = \frac{400 \text{ apples}}{\text{hr}}$

Now set up an equation to find the time it takes to pick 1000 apples:

$$\text{total time} = \frac{1 \text{ hr}}{400 \text{ apples}} \times 1000 \text{ apples} = \frac{1000}{400} \text{ hrs} = \textbf{2.5 hrs}$$

COORDINATE GEOMETRY

Coordinate geometry is the study of points, lines, and shapes that have been graphed on a set of axes.

Points, Lines, and Planes

In coordinate geometry, points are plotted on a **COORDINATE PLANE**, a two-dimensional plane in which the x-axis indicates horizontal direction and the y-axis indicates vertical direction. The intersection of these two axes is the origin. Points are defined by their location in relation to the horizontal and vertical axes. The coordinates of a point are written (x, y). The coordinates of the origin are $(0, 0)$. The x coordinates to the right of the origin and the y-coordinates above it are positive; the x-coordinates to the left of the origin and the y-coordinates below it are negative.

A line is formed by connecting any two points on a coordinate plane; lines are continuous in both directions. Lines can be defined by their slope, or steepness, and their y-intercept, or the point at which they intersect the y-axis. A line is represented by the equation $y = mx + b$. The constant m represents slope and the constant b represents the y-intercept.

Examples

1. Matt parks his car near a forest where he goes hiking. From his car he hikes 1 mile north, 2 miles east, then 3 miles west. If his car represents the origin, find the coordinates of Matt's current location.

   To find the coordinates, you must find Matt's displacement along the x- and y-axes. Matt hiked 1 mile north and zero miles south, so his displacement along the y-axis is +1 mile. Matt hiked 2 miles east and 3 miles west, so his displacement along the x axis is +2 miles − 3 miles = −1 mile.

   Matt's coordinates are (−1, 1).

2. A square is drawn on a coordinate plane. The bottom corners are located at (−2, 3) and (4, 3). What are the coordinates for the top right corner?

   Draw the coordinate plane and plot the given points. If you connect these points you will see that the bottom side is 6 units long. Since it is a square, all sides must be 6 units long. Count 6 units up from the point (4, 3) to find the top right corner.

   The coordinates for the top right corner are (4, 9).

The Distance and Midpoint Formulas

To determine the distance between the points (x_1, y_1) and (x_2, y_2) from a grid use the formula $d = \sqrt{(x_2 - x_1)^2 + (y_2 - y_1)^2}$. The midpoint, which is halfway between the 2 points, is the point $\left(\frac{x_1 + x_2}{2}, \frac{y_1 + y_2}{2}\right)$.

Examples

1. What is the distance between points (3, −6) and (−5, 2)?

   Plug the values for $x_1, x_2, y_1,$ and y_2 into the distance formula and simplify:

   $$d = \sqrt{(-5 - 3)^2 + (2 - (-6))^2} = \sqrt{64 + 64} = \sqrt{64 \times 2} = \mathbf{8\sqrt{2}}$$

2. What is the midpoint between points (3, −6) and (−5, 2)?

   Plug the values for $x_1, x_2, y_1,$ and y_2 into the midpoint formula and simplify:

   $$\text{midpoint} = \left(\frac{-5 + 3}{2}, \frac{2 + -6}{2}\right) = \left(\frac{-2)}{2}, \frac{4}{2}\right) = \mathbf{(-1, 2)}$$

READING

The PERT Reading section assesses your ability to summarize, interpret, and draw conclusions about both non-fiction and fiction passages. On the test, you will read both types of passages; specific questions may ask about the following:

- the main idea of a passage
- the role of supporting details in a passage
- adding supporting details to a passage
- the structure of a passage
- the author's purpose
- logical inferences that can be drawn from a passage
- comparing passages
- vocabulary and figurative language

The questions more broadly fall under four general question types:

MAIN IDEA: A question may directly or indirectly ask you about the main idea of a passage. Summarizing it briefly in your own words or reviewing the first few paragraphs will help you identify the main idea and narrow down your answer choices.

ABOUT THE AUTHOR: These questions ask about the author's attitude, thoughts, and opinions. To determine the correct response, pay attention to context clues in the text. The answer may not be explicitly stated but instead conveyed in the overall message.

PASSAGE FACTS: To answer these questions correctly, you must distinguish between facts and opinions presented in the passage. You may also be asked to identify specific information provided by the author.

ADDITIONAL INFORMATION: These questions ask you to consider what information could be added to or was missing from the passage; they may even provide a fill-in-the-blank option to include a new statement at a certain point in the text. Keep in mind that any additional information should strengthen the author's argument. These questions may also ask in what direction the passage was going; that is, about logical inferences that can be drawn from the text.

STRATEGIES

Despite the different types of questions you will face, there are some strategies for Reading Comprehension that always apply:

- Read the questions before reading the passage. You will save time, as you will know what to look out for as you read.
- Use the process of elimination. Often at least one answer choice in a question is obviously incorrect. After reading the passage, eliminate any blatantly incorrect answer choices to increase your chances of finding the correct answer much more quickly.
- Avoid negative statements. Correct responses tend to be neutral or positive, so if it seems like an answer choice has a negative connotation, it is very likely that the answer is intentionally false.

THE MAIN IDEA

The main idea of a text is the author's purpose in writing a book, article, story, etc. Being able to identify and understand the main idea is a critical skill necessary to comprehend and appreciate what you're reading.

Consider a political election. A candidate is running for office and plans to deliver a speech asserting her position on tax reform. The topic of the speech—tax reform—is clear to voters, and probably of interest to many. However, imagine that the candidate believes that taxes should be lowered. She is likely to assert this argument in her speech, supporting it with examples proving why lowering taxes would benefit the public and how it could be accomplished. While the topic of the speech would be tax reform, the benefit of lowering taxes would be the main idea. Other candidates may have different perspectives on the topic; they may believe that higher taxes are necessary, or that current taxes are adequate. It is likely that their speeches, while on the same topic of tax reform, would have different main ideas: different arguments likewise supported by different examples. Determining what a speaker, writer, or text is asserting about a specific issue will reveal the main idea.

One more quick note: the exam may also ask about a passage's theme, which is similar to but distinct from its topic. While a topic is usually a specific person, place, thing, or issue, the theme is an idea or concept that the author refers back to frequently. Examples of common themes include ideas like the importance of family, the dangers of technology, and the beauty of nature.

There will be many questions on the exam that require you to differentiate between the topic, theme, and main idea of a passage. Let's look at an example:

Babe Didrikson Zaharias, one of the most decorated female athletes of the twentieth century, is an inspiration for everyone. Born in 1911 in Beaumont, Texas, Zaharias lived in a time when women were considered second-class to men, but she never let that stop her from becoming a champion. Babe was one of seven children in a poor immigrant family, and was competitive from an early age. As a child she excelled at most things she tried, especially sports, which continued into high school and beyond. After high school, Babe played amateur basketball for two years, and soon after began training in track and field. Despite the fact that women were only allowed to enter in three events, Babe represented the United States in the 1932 Los Angeles Olympics, and won two gold medals and one silver for track and field events.

In the early 1930s, Babe began playing golf which earned her a legacy. The first tournament she entered was a men's only tournament; however she did not make the cut to play. Playing golf as an amateur was the only option for a woman at this time, since there was no professional women's league. Babe played as an amateur for a little over a decade, until she turned pro in 1947 for the Ladies Professional Golf Association (LPGA) of which she was a founding member. During her career as a golfer, Babe won eighty-two tournaments, amateur and professional, including the U.S. Women's Open, All-American Open, and British Women's Open Golf Tournament. In 1953, Babe was diagnosed with cancer, but fourteen weeks later, she played in a tournament. That year she won her third U.S.

Women's Open. However by 1955, she didn't have the physicality to compete anymore, and she died of the disease in 1956.

The topic of this passage is obviously Babe Zaharias—the whole passage describes events from her life. Determining the main idea, however, requires a little more analysis. The passage describes Babe Zaharias' life, but the main idea of the paragraph is what it says *about* her life. To figure out the main idea, consider what the writer is saying about Babe Zaharias. The writer is saying that she's someone to admire—that's the main idea and what unites all the information in the paragraph. Lastly, what might the theme of the passage be? The writer refers to several broad concepts, including never giving up and overcoming the odds, both of which could be themes for the passage. Two major indicators of the main idea of a paragraph or passage follow below:

- It is a general idea; it applies to all the more specific ideas in the passage. Every other sentence in a paragraph should be able to relate in some way to the main idea.

- It asserts a specific viewpoint that the author supports with facts, opinions, or other details. In other words, the main idea takes a stand.

Example

From so far away it's easy to imagine the surface of our solar system's planets as enigmas—how could we ever know what those far-flung planets really look like? It turns out, however, that scientists have a number of tools at their disposal that allow them to paint detailed pictures of many planets' surfaces. The topography of Venus, for example, has been explored by several space probes, including the Russian Venera landers and NASA's Magellan orbiter. These craft used imaging and radar to map the surface of the planet, identifying a whole host of features including volcanoes, craters, and a complex system of channels. Mars has similarly been mapped by space probes, including the famous Mars Rovers, which are automated vehicles that actually landed on the surface of Mars. These rovers have been used by NASA and other space agencies to study the geology, climate, and possible biology of the planet.

In addition these long-range probes, NASA has also used its series of orbiting telescopes to study distant planets. These four massively powerful telescopes include the famous Hubble Space Telescope as well as the Compton Gamma Ray Observatory, Chandra X-Ray Observatory, and the Spitzer Space Telescope. Scientists can use these telescopes to examine planets using not only visible light but also infrared and near-infrared light, ultraviolet light, x-rays and gamma rays.

Powerful telescopes aren't just found in space: NASA makes use of Earth-bound telescopes as well. Scientists at the

National Radio Astronomy Observatory in Charlottesville, VA, have spent decades using radio imaging to build an incredibly detailed portrait of Venus' surface. In fact, Earth-bound telescopes offer a distinct advantage over orbiting telescopes because they allow scientists to capture data from a fixed point, which in turn allows them to effectively compare data collected over long period of time.

Which of the following sentences best describes the main idea of the passage?

A) It's impossible to know what the surfaces of other planets are really like.

B) Telescopes are an important tool for scientists studying planets in our solar system.

C) Venus' surface has many of the same features as the Earth's, including volcanoes, craters, and channels.

D) Scientists use a variety of advanced technologies to study the surface of the planets in our solar system.

Answer A) can be eliminated because it directly contradicts the rest of the passage. Answers B) and C) can also be eliminated because they offer only specific details from the passage—while both choices contain details from the passage, neither is general enough to encompass the passage as a whole. **Only answer D) provides an assertion that is both backed up by the passage's content and general enough to cover the entire passage.**

Topic and Summary Sentences

The main idea of a paragraph usually appears within the TOPIC SENTENCE. The topic sentence introduces the main idea to readers; it indicates not only the topic of a passage, but also the writer's perspective on the topic. Notice, for example, how the first sentence in the example paragraph about Babe Zaharias states the main idea: *Babe Didrikson Zaharias, one of the most decorated female athletes of the twentieth century, is an inspiration for everyone.*

Even though paragraphs generally begin with topic sentences due to their introductory nature, on occasion writers build up to the topic sentence by using supporting details in order to generate interest or build an argument. Be alert for paragraphs when writers do not include a clear topic sentence at all; even without a clear topic sentence, a paragraph will still have a main idea. You may also see a SUMMARY SENTENCE at the end of a passage. As its name suggests, this sentence sums up the passage, often by restating the main idea and the author's key evidence supporting it.

Example

In the following paragraph, what are the topic and summary sentences?

The Constitution of the United States establishes a series of limits to rein in centralized power. Separation of powers distributes federal authority among three competing branches: the executive, the legislative, and the judicial. Checks and balances allow the branches to check the usurpation of power by any one branch. States' rights are protected under the Constitution from too much encroachment by the federal government. Enumeration of powers names the specific and few powers the federal government has. These four restrictions have helped sustain the American republic for over two centuries.

The topic sentence is the first sentence in the paragraph. It introduces the topic of discussion, in this case the constitutional limits aimed at resisting centralized power. **The summary sentence is the last sentence in the paragraph.** It sums up the information that was just presented: here, that constitutional limits have helped sustain the United States of America for over two hundred years.

Implied Main Idea

A paragraph without a clear topic sentence still has a main idea; rather than clearly stated, it is implied. Determining the IMPLIED MAIN IDEA requires some detective work: you will need to look at the author's word choice and tone in addition to the content of the passage to find his or her main idea. Let's look at an example paragraph.

Examples

One of my summer reading books was *Mockingjay*. Though it's several hundred pages long, I read it in just a few days. I was captivated by the adventures of the main character and the complicated plot of the book. However, I felt like the ending didn't reflect the excitement of the story. Given what a powerful personality the main character has, I felt like the ending didn't do her justice.

Even without a clear topic sentence, this paragraph has a main idea. What is the writer's perspective on the book—what is the writer saying about it?

A) *Mockingjay* is a terrific novel.

B) *Mockingjay* is disappointing.

C) *Mockingjay* is full of suspense.

D) *Mockingjay* is a lousy novel.

The correct answer is B): the novel is disappointing. The process of elimination will reveal the correct answer if that is not immediately clear. While that the paragraph begins with positive commentary on the book—I was captivated by the adventures of the main character and the complicated plot of the book—this positive idea is followed by the contradictory transition word however. A) cannot be the correct answer because the author concludes that the novel was poor. Likewise, D) cannot be correct because it does not encompass all the ideas in the paragraph; despite the negative conclusion, the author enjoyed most of the book. The main idea should

Understanding the tone of a passage can help you quickly eliminate answer choices.

be able to encompass all of the thoughts in a paragraph; choice D) does not apply to the beginning of this paragraph. Finally, choice C) is too specific; it could only apply to the brief description of the plot and adventures of the main character. That leaves choice B) as the best option. The author initially enjoyed the book, but was disappointed by the ending, which seemed unworthy of the exciting plot and character.

Fortunately, none of Alyssa's coworkers has ever seen inside the large filing drawer in her desk. Disguised by the meticulous neatness of the rest of her workspace, there was no sign of the chaos beneath. To even open it, she had to struggle for several minutes with the enormous pile of junk jamming the drawer, until it would suddenly give way, and papers, folders, and candy wrappers spilled out of the top and onto the floor. It was an organizational nightmare, with torn notes and spreadsheets haphazardly thrown on top of each other, and melted candy smeared across pages. She was worried the odor would soon permeate to her coworker's desks, revealing to them her secret.

Which of the following expresses the main idea of this paragraph?

A) Alyssa wishes she could move to a new desk.

B) Alyssa wishes she had her own office.

C) Alyssa is glad none of her coworkers know about her messy drawer.

D) Alyssa is sad because she doesn't have any coworkers.

What the paragraph adds up to is that Alyssa is terribly embarrassed about her messy drawer, and she's glad that none of her coworkers have seen it, making C) the correct answer choice. This is the main idea. The paragraph opens with the word *fortunately*, so we know that she thinks it's a good thing that none of her coworkers have seen inside the drawer. Plus, notice how the drawer is described: *it was an organizational nightmare*, and it apparently doesn't even function properly: *to even open the drawer, she had to struggle for several minutes*. The writer reveals that it has an odor, with *melted candy* inside. Alyssa is clearly ashamed of her drawer and worries about what her coworkers would think if they saw inside it.

SUPPORTING DETAILS

SUPPORTING DETAILS provide more support for the author's main idea. For instance, in the Babe Zaharias example, the writer makes the general assertion that *Babe Didrikson Zaharias, one of the most decorated female athletes of the twentieth century, is an inspiration for everyone.* The other sentences offer specific facts and details that prove why she is an inspiration: the names of the illnesses she overcame, and the specific years she competed in the Olympics.

SIGNAL WORDS
- For example
- Specifically
- In addition
- Furthermore
- For instance
- Others
- In particular
- Some

Writers often provide clues that can help you identify supporting details. These **SIGNAL WORDS** tell you that a supporting fact or idea will follow, and so can be helpful in identifying supporting details. Signal words can also help you rule out sentences that are not the main idea or topic sentence: if a sentence begins with one of these phrases, it will likely be too specific to be a main idea.

Examples

From so far away it's easy to imagine the surface of our solar system's planets as enigmas—how could we ever know what those far-flung planets really look like? It turns out, however, that scientists have a number of tools at their disposal that allow them to paint detailed pictures of many planets' surfaces. The topography of Venus, for example, has been explored by several space probes, including the Russian Venera landers and NASA's Magellan orbiter. These craft used imaging and radar to map the surface of the planet, identifying a whole host of features including volcanoes, craters, and a complex system of channels. Mars has similarly been mapped by space probes, including the famous Mars Rovers, which are automated vehicles that actually landed on the surface of Mars. These rovers have been used by NASA and other space agencies to study the geology, climate, and possible biology of the planet.

In addition to these long-range probes, NASA has also used its series of orbiting telescopes to study distant planets. These four massively powerful telescopes include the famous Hubble Space Telescope as well as the Compton Gamma Ray Observatory, Chandra X-Ray Observatory, and the Spitzer Space Telescope. Scientists can use these telescopes to examine planets using not only visible light but also infrared and near-infrared light, ultraviolet light, x-rays and gamma rays.

Powerful telescopes aren't just found in space: NASA makes use of Earth-bound telescopes as well. Scientists at the National Radio Astronomy Observatory in Charlottesville, VA, have spent decades using radio imaging to build an incredibly detailed portrait of Venus' surface. In fact, Earth-bound telescopes offer a distinct advantage over orbiting telescopes because they allow scientists to capture data from a fixed point, which in turn allows them to effectively compare data collected over long period of time.

1. Which sentence from the text best helps develop the idea that scientists make use of many different technologies to study the surfaces of other planets?

   A) These rovers have been used by NASA and other space agencies to study the geology, climate, and possible biology of the planet.

   B) From so far away it's easy to imagine the surface of our solar system's planets as enigmas—how could we ever know what those far-flung planets really look like?

   C) In addition these long-range probes, NASA has also used its series of orbiting telescopes to study distant planets.

   D) These craft used imaging and radar to map the surface of the planet, identifying a whole host of features including volcanoes, craters, and a complex system of channels.

   You're looking for detail from the passage that supports the main idea—scientists make use of many different technologies to study the surfaces of other planets. Answer A) includes a specific detail about rovers, but does not offer any details that support the idea of multiple technologies being used. Similarly, answer D) provides another specific detail about space probes. Answer B) doesn't provide any supporting details; it simply introduces the topic of the passage. **Only answer C) provides a detail that directly supports the author's assertion that scientists use multiple technologies to study the planets.**

2. If true, which detail could be added to the passage above to support the author's argument that scientists use many different technologies to study the surface of planets?

   A) Because the Earth's atmosphere blocks x-rays, gamma rays, and infrared radiation, NASA needed to put telescopes in orbit above the atmosphere.

   B) In 2015, NASA released a map of Venus which was created by compiling images from orbiting telescopes and long-range space probes.

   C) NASA is currently using the Curiosity and Opportunity rovers to look for signs of ancient life on Mars.

   D) NASA has spent over $2.5 billion to build, launch, and repair the Hubble Space Telescope.

   You can eliminate answers C) and D) because they don't address the topic of studying the surface of planets. Answer A) can also be eliminated because it only addresses a single technology. **Only choice B) would add support to the author's claim about the importance of using multiple technologies.**

CONTINUE

3. The author likely included the detail *Earth-bound telescopes offer a distinct advantage over orbiting telescopes because they allow scientists to capture data from a fixed point* in order to:

A) Explain why it has taken scientists so long to map the surface of Venus.

B) Suggest that Earth-bound telescopes are the most important equipment used by NASA scientists.

C) Prove that orbiting telescopes will soon be replaced by Earth-bound telescopes.

D) Demonstrate why NASA scientists rely on many different types of scientific equipment.

Only answer D) speaks directly to the author's main argument. The author doesn't mention how long it has taken to map the surface of Venus (answer A), nor does he say that one technology is more important than the others (answer B). And while this detail does highlight the advantages of using Earth-bound telescopes, the author's argument is that many technologies are being used at the same time, so there's no reason to think that orbiting telescopes will be replaced (answer C).

TEXT STRUCTURE

Authors can structure passages in a number of different ways. These distinct organizational patterns, referred to as TEXT STRUCTURE, use the logical relationships between ideas to improve the readability and coherence of a text. The most common ways passages are organized include:

- **PROBLEM-SOLUTION**: the author presents a problem and then discusses a solution.
- **COMPARISON-CONTRAST**: the author presents two situations and then discusses the similarities and differences.
- **CAUSE-EFFECT**: the author presents an action and then discusses the resulting effects.
- **DESCRIPTIVE**: an idea, object, person, or other item is described in detail.

Example

The issue of public transportation has begun to haunt the fast-growing cities of the southern United States. Unlike their northern counterparts, cities like Atlanta, Dallas, and Houston have long promoted growth out and not up—these are cities full of sprawling suburbs and single-family homes, not densely concentrated skyscrapers and apartments. What to do then, when all those suburbanites need to get into the central business districts for work? For a long time it seemed highways were the answer: twenty-lane wide expanses of concrete that would allow commuters to move from home to work and back again. But these modern miracles have become time-sucking, pollution-spewing nightmares. They may not like it, but it's time for these cities to turn toward public transport like trains and buses if they want their cities to remain livable.

The organization of this passage can best be described as:

A) a comparison of two similar ideas

B) a description of a place

C) a discussion of several effects all related to the same cause

D) a discussion of a problem followed by the suggestion of a solution

You can exclude answer choice C) because the author provides no root cause or a list of effects. From there this question gets tricky, because the passage contains structures similar to those described above. For example, it compares two things (cities in the North and South) and describes a place (a sprawling city). However, if you look at the overall organization of the passage, you can see that it starts by presenting a problem (transportation) and then presents a solution (trains and buses), making **answer D) the only choice that encompasses the entire passage.**

THE AUTHOR'S PURPOSE

Whenever an author writes a text, she always has a purpose, whether that's to entertain, inform, explain, or persuade. A short story, for example, is meant to entertain, while an online news article would be designed to inform the public about a current event.

Each of these different types of writing has a specific name. On the exam, you may be asked to identify which of these categories a passage fits into either by name or by general purpose:

- Narrative writing tells a story (novel, short story, play).
- Expository writing informs people (newspaper and magazine articles).
- Technical writing explains something (product manual, directions).
- Persuasive writing tries to convince the reader of something (opinion column on a blog).

You may also be asked about primary and secondary sources. These terms describe not the writing itself but the author's relationship to the topic. A primary source is an unaltered piece of writing that was composed during the time when the events being described took place; these texts are often written by the people involved. A secondary source might address the same topic but provides extra commentary or analysis. These texts can be written by people not directly involved in the events. For example, a book written by a political candidate to inform people about his or her stand on an issue is a primary source; an online article written by a journalist analyzing how that position will affect the election is a secondary source.

Example

Elizabeth closed her eyes and braced herself on the armrests that divided her from her fellow passengers. Take-off was always the worst part for her. The revving of the engines, the way her stomach dropped as the plane lurched upward: it made her feel sick. Then, she had to watch the world fade away beneath her, getting smaller and smaller until it was just her and the clouds hurtling through the sky. Sometimes (but only sometimes) it just had to be endured, though. She focused on the thought of her sister's smiling face and her new baby nephew as the plane slowly pulled onto the runway.

The passage above is reflective of which type of writing?

A) narrative

B) expository

C) technical

D) persuasive

The passage is telling a story—we meet Elizabeth and learn about her fear of flying—so it's a narrative text. There is no factual information presented or explained, nor is the author trying to persuade the reader.

FACTS VS. OPINIONS

On PERT Reading passages you might be asked to identify a statement in a passage as either a fact or an opinion, so you'll need to know the difference between the two. A **FACT** is a statement or thought that can be proven to be true. The statement *Wednesday comes after Tuesday* is a fact—you can point to a calendar to prove it. In contrast, an **OPINION** is an assumption that is not based in fact and cannot be proven to be true. The assertion that *television is more entertaining than feature films* is an opinion—people will disagree on this, and there's no reference you can use to prove or disprove it.

✔──────────

Which of the following words would be associated with opinions?

- for example . . .
- studies have shown . . .
- I believe . . .
- in fact . . .
- the best/worst . . .
- it's possible that . .

Example

Exercise is critical for healthy development in children. Today, there is an epidemic of unhealthy children in the United States who will face health problems in adulthood due to poor diet and lack of exercise as children. This is a problem for all Americans, especially with the rising cost of healthcare.

It is vital that school systems and parents encourage their children to engage in a minimum of thirty minutes of cardiovascular exercise each day, mildly increasing their heart rate for a sustained period. This is proven to decrease the likelihood of developmental diabetes, obesity, and a multitude of other health problems. Also, children need a proper diet rich in fruits and vegetables so that they can grow and develop physically, as well as learn healthy eating habits early on.

Which of the following is a fact in the passage, not an opinion?

A) Fruits and vegetables are the best way to help children be healthy.

B) Children today are lazier than they were in previous generations.

C) The risk of diabetes in children is reduced by physical activity.

D) Children should engage in thirty minutes of exercise a day.

Keep an eye out for answer choices that may be facts, but which are not stated or discussed in the passage.

Choice B) can be discarded immediately because it is negative and is not discussed anywhere in the passage. Answers A) and D) are both opinions—the author is promoting exercise, fruits, and vegetables as a way to make children healthy. (Notice that these incorrect answers contain words that hint at being an opinion such as *best, should*, or other comparisons.) **Answer B), on the other hand, is a simple fact stated by the author; it's introduced by the word *proven* to indicate that you don't need to just take the author's word for it.**

Drawing Conclusions

In addition to understanding the main idea and factual content of a passage, you'll also be asked to take your analysis one step further and anticipate what other information could logically be added to the passage. In a non-fiction passage, for example, you might be asked which statement the author of the passage would agree with. In an excerpt from a fictional work, you might be asked to anticipate what the character would do next.

To answer these questions, you need to have a solid understanding of the topic, theme, and main idea of the passage; armed with this information, you can figure out which of the answer choices best fits within those criteria (or alternatively, which ones do not). For example, if the author of the passage is advocating for safer working conditions in textile factories, any supporting details that would be added to the passage should support that idea. You might add sentences that contain information about the number of accidents that occur in textile factories or that outline a new plan for fire safety.

Examples

Today, there is an epidemic of unhealthy children in the United States who will face health problems in adulthood due to poor diet and lack of exercise during their childhood. This is a problem for all Americans, as adults with chronic health issues are adding to the rising cost of healthcare. A child who grows up living an unhealthy lifestyle is likely to become an adult who does the same.

Because exercise is critical for healthy development in children, it is vital that school systems and parents encourage their children to engage in a minimum of thirty minutes of cardiovascular exercise each day. Even this small amount of exercise has been proven to decrease the likelihood that young people will develop diabetes, obesity, and other health issues as adults. In addition to exercise, children need a proper diet rich in fruits and vegetables so that they can grow and develop physically. Starting a good diet early also teaches children healthy eating habits they will carry into adulthood.

1. The author of this passage would most likely agree with which statement?

   A) Parents are solely responsible for the health of their children.

   B) Children who do not want to exercise should not be made to.

   C) Improved childhood nutrition will help lower the amount Americans spend on healthcare.

   D) It's not important to teach children healthy eating habits because they will learn them as adults.

The author would most likely support answer C): he mentions in the first paragraph that unhealthy habits are adding to the rising cost of healthcare. The main idea of the passage is that nutrition and exercise are important for children, so answer B) doesn't make sense—the author would likely support measures to encourage children to exercise. Answers A) and D) can also be eliminated because they are directly contradicted in the text. The author specifically mentions the role of schools systems, so he doesn't believe parents are solely responsible for their children's health. He also specifically states that children who grow up with unhealthy habit will become adults with unhealthy habits, which
contradicts D).

Elizabeth closed her eyes and braced herself on the armrests that divided her from her fellow passengers. Take-off was always the worst part for her. The revving of the engines, the way her stomach dropped as the plane lurched upward: it made her feel sick. Then, she had to watch the world fade away beneath her, getting smaller and smaller until it was just her and the clouds hurtling through the sky. Sometimes (but only sometimes) it just had to be endured,
though. She focused on the thought of her sister's smiling face and her new baby nephew as the plane slowly pulled onto the runway.

2. Which of the following is Elizabeth least likely to do in the future?

   A) Take a flight to her brother's wedding.

   B) Apply for a job as a flight attendant.

   C) Never board an airplane again.

   D) Get sick on an airplane.

It's clear from the passage that Elizabeth hates flying, but it willing to endure it for the sake of visiting her family. Thus, it seems likely that she would be willing to get on a plane for her brother's wedding, making A) and C) incorrect answers. The passage also explicitly tells us that she feels sick on planes, so D) is likely to happen. **We can infer, though, that she would not enjoy being on an airplane for work, so she's very unlikely to apply for a job as a flight attendant, which is choice B).**

MEANING OF WORDS AND PHRASES

On the Reading section you may also be asked to provide definitions or intended meanings for words within passages. You may have never encountered some of these words before the test, but there are tricks you can use to figure out what they mean.

Context Clues

The most fundamental vocabulary skill is using the context in which a word is used to determine its meaning. Your ability to observe sentences closely is extremely useful when it comes to understanding new vocabulary words.

There are two types of context that can help you understand the meaning of unfamiliar words: situational context and sentence context. Regardless of which context is present, these types of questions are not really testing your knowledge of vocabulary; rather, they test your ability to comprehend the meaning of a word through its usage.

SITUATIONAL CONTEXT is context that is presented by the setting or circumstances in which a word or phrase occurs. **SENTENCE CONTEXT** occurs within the specific sentence that contains the vocabulary word. To figure out words using sentence context clues, you should first determine the most important words in the sentence.

There are four types of clues that can help you understand context, and therefore the meaning of a word:

- **RESTATEMENT** clues occur when the definition of the word is clearly stated in the sentence.
- **POSITIVE/NEGATIVE CLUES** can tell you whether a word has a positive or negative meaning.
- **CONTRAST CLUES** include the opposite meaning of a word. Words like *but, on the other hand*, and *however* are tip-offs that a sentence contains a contrast clue.
- **SPECIFIC DETAIL CLUES** provide a precise detail that can help you understand the meaning of the word.

It is important to remember that more than one of these clues can be present in the same sentence. The more there are, the easier it will be to determine the meaning of the word. For example, the following sentence uses both restatement and positive/negative clues: *Janet suddenly found herself destitute, so poor she could barely afford to eat.* The second part of the sentence clearly indicates that *destitute* is a negative word. It also restates the meaning: very poor.

Examples

Select the answer that most closely matches the definition of the underlined word or phrase as it is used in the sentence.

1. I had a hard time reading her <u>illegible</u> handwriting.

   A) neat

   B) unsafe

   C) sloppy

   D) educated

   Already, you know that this sentence is discussing something that is hard to read. Look at the word that illegible is describing: handwriting. Based on context clues, you can tell that illegible means that her handwriting is hard to read.

   Next, look at the answer choices. Choice A), *neat*, is obviously a wrong answer because neat handwriting would not be difficult to read. Choices B) and D), *unsafe* and *educated*, don't make sense. **Therefore, choice C), *sloppy*, is the best answer.**

2. The dog was <u>dauntless</u> in the face of danger, braving the fire to save the girl trapped inside the building.

   A) difficult

   B) fearless

   C) imaginative

   D) startled

   Demonstrating bravery in the face of danger would be B) fearless. In this case, the restatement clue (braving the fire) tells you exactly what the word means.

3. Beth did not spend any time preparing for the test, but Tyrone kept a <u>rigorous</u> study schedule.

   A) strict

   B) loose

   C) boring

   D) strange

   In this case, the contrast word *but* tells us that Tyrone studied in a different way than Beth, which means it's a contrast clue. If Beth did not study hard, then Tyrone did. **The best answer, therefore, is choice A).**

Analyzing Words

As you no doubt know, determining the meaning of a word can be more complicated than just looking in a dictionary. A word might have more than one DENOTATION, or definition; which one the author intends can only be judged by looking at the surrounding text. For example, the word *quack* can refer to the sound a duck makes, or to a person who publicly pretends to have a qualification which he or she does not actually possess.

A word may also have different CONNOTATIONS, which are the implied meanings and emotion a word evokes in the reader. For example, a cubicle is a simply a walled desk in an office, but for many the word implies a constrictive, uninspiring workplace. Connotations can vary greatly between cultures and even between individuals.

Lastly, authors might make use of FIGURATIVE LANGUAGE, which is the use of a word to imply something other than the word's literal definition. This is often done by comparing two things. If you say *I felt like a butterfly when I got a new haircut*, the listener knows you don't resemble an insect but instead felt beautiful and transformed.

Examples

Select the answer that most closely matches the definition of the underlined word or phrase as it is used in the sentence.

1. The uneven <u>pupils</u> suggested that brain damage was possible.

   A) part of the eye

   B) student in a classroom

   C) walking pace

   D) breathing sounds

   Only answer choice A (part of the eye) matches both the definition of the word and context of the sentence. Choice B is an alternative definition for pupil, but does make sense in the sentence. Both C and D could be correct in the context of the sentence, but neither is a definition of pupil.

2. Aiden examined the antique lamp and worried that he had been <u>taken for a ride</u>. He had paid a lot for the vintage lamp, but it looked like it was worthless.

   A) transported

   B) forgotten

   C) deceived

   D) hindered

   It's clear from the context of the sentence that Aiden was not literally taken for a ride. Instead, this phrase is an example of figurative language. **From context clues it can be figured out that Aiden paid too much for the lamp, so he was deceived (answer choice C).**

→

CONTINUE

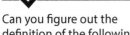

Can you figure out the definition of the following words using their parts?

- ambidextrous
- anthropology
- egocentric
- diagram
- hemisphere
- homicide
- metamorphosis
- nonsense
- portable
- rewind
- submarine
- triangle
- unicycle

Word Structure

Although you are not expected to know every word in the English language for your test, you will need the ability to use deductive reasoning to find the choice that is the best match for the word in question, which is why we are going to explain how to break a word into its parts to determine its meaning. Many words can be broken down into three main parts:

PREFIX — ROOT — SUFFIX

ROOTS are the building blocks of all words. Every word is either a root itself or has a root. Just as a plant cannot grow without roots, neither can vocabulary, because a word must have a root to give it meaning. The root is what is left when you strip away all the prefixes and suffixes from a word. For example, in the word *unclear*, if you take away the prefix *un-*, you have the root *clear*.

Roots are not always recognizable words, because they generally come from Latin or Greek words, such as *nat*, a Latin root meaning born. The word *native*, which means a person born in a referenced placed, comes from this root, so does the word *prenatal*, meaning before birth. It's important to keep in mind, however, that roots do not always match the exact definitions of words, and they can have several different spellings.

PREFIXES are syllables added to the beginning of a word and **SUFFIXES** are syllables added to the end of the word. Both carry assigned meanings and can be attached to a word to completely change the word's meaning or to enhance the word's original meaning.

Let's use the word prefix itself as an example: *fix* means to place something securely and *pre-* means before. Therefore, *prefix* means to place something before or in front. Now let's look at a suffix: in the word *feminism*, *femin* is a root which means female. The suffix *-ism* means act, practice, or process. Thus, *feminism* is the process of establishing equal rights for women.

Although you cannot determine the meaning of a word by a prefix or suffix alone, you can use this knowledge to eliminate answer choices; understanding whether the word is positive or negative can give you the partial meaning of the word.

Table 2.1. Common roots and affixes

ROOT	DEFINITION	EXAMPLE
ast(er)	star	asteroid, astronomy
audi	hear	audience, audible
auto	self	automatic, autograph
bene	good	beneficent, benign
bio	life	biology, biorhythm
chrono	time	chronometer, chronic
dict	say	dictionary, dictation
duc	lead or make	ductile, produce
gen	give birth	generation, genetics
geo	earth	geography, geometry
graph	write	graphical, autograph
jur or jus	law	justice, jurisdiction
log or logue	thought	logic, logarithm
luc	light	lucidity
man	hand	manual
mand	order	remand
mis	send	transmission
path	feel	pathology
phil	love	philanthropy
phon	sound	phonograph
port	carry	export
qui	quiet	quiet
scrib or script	write	scribe, transcript
sense or sent	feel	sentiment
tele	far away	telephone
terr	earth	terrace
vac	empty	vacant
vid	see	video
vis	see	vision
omni	all	omnivores
cap	take	capture
ced	yield	secede
corp	body	corporeal
demo	people	democracy
grad	step	graduate
crac or crat	rule	autocrat
mono	one	monotone
uni	single	Unicode
ject	throw	eject

CONTINUE

Table 2.2. Common prefixes

PREFIX	DEFINITION	EXAMPLE
a- (also an-)	not, without; to, towards; of, completely	atheist, anaemic, aside, aback, anew, abashed
ante-	before, preceding	antecedent, ante-room
anti-	opposing, against	antibiotic, anticlimax
com- (also co-, col-, con-, cor-)	with, jointly, completely	combat, codriver, collude, confide
dis- (also di-)	negation, removal	disadvantage, disbar
en- (also em-)	put into or on; bring into the condition of; intensify	engulf, entomb
hypo-	under	hypoglycemic, hypothermia
in- (also il-, im-, ir-)	not, without; in, into, towards, inside	infertile, impossible, influence, include
intra-	inside, within	intravenous, intrapersonal
out-	surpassing, exceeding; external, away from	outperform, outdoor
over-	excessively, completely; upper, outer, over, above	overconfident, overcast
pre-	before	precondition, pre-adolescent, prelude
re-	again	reapply, remake
semi-	half, partly	semicircle, semi-conscious
syn- (also sym-)	in union, acting together	symmetry, symbiotic
trans-	across, beyond	transatlantic
trans-	into a different state	translate
under-	beneath, below	underarm, undersecretary
under-	not enough	underdeveloped

Examples

Select the answer that most closely matches the definition of the underlined word or phrase as it is used in the sentence.

1. The <u>bellicose</u> dog will be sent to training school next week.

    A) misbehaved

    B) friendly

    C) scared

    D) aggressive

Both misbehaved and aggressive look like possible answers given the context of the sentence. **However, the prefix *belli*, which means warlike, can be used to confirm that aggressive (choice D) is the right answer.**

2. The new menu <u>rejuvenated</u> the restaurant and made it one of the most popular spots in town.

    A) established

    B) invigorated

    C) improved

    D) motivated

All of the answer choices could make sense in the context of the sentence, so it's necessary to use word structure to find the definition. The root *juven* means young and the prefix *re* means again, so rejuvenate means to be made young again. **The answer choice with the most similar meanings is *invigorated*, which means to give something energy.**

COMPARING PASSAGES

In addition to analyzing single passages, the [exam] will also require you to compare two passages. Usually these passages will discuss the same topic, and it will be your task to identify the similarities and differences between the authors' main ideas, supporting details, and tones.

Examples

Read the following two passages and answer the following questions.

Passage 1

Today, there is an epidemic of unhealthy children in the United States who will face health problems in adulthood due to poor diet and lack of exercise during their childhoods: in 2012, the Centers for Disease Control found that 18 percent of students aged 6-11 were obese. This is a problem for all Americans, as adults with chronic health issues are adding to the rising cost of healthcare. A child who grows up living an unhealthy lifestyle is likely to become an adult who does the same.

Because exercise is critical for healthy development in children, it is vital that school systems and parents encourage their children to engage in a minimum of thirty minutes of cardiovascular exercise each day. Even this small amount of exercise has been proven to decrease the likelihood that young people will develop diabetes, obesity, and other health issues as adults. In addition to exercise, children need a proper diet rich in fruits and vegetables so that they can grow and develop physically. Starting a good diet early also teaches children healthy eating habits they will carry into adulthood.

Passage 2

When was the last time you took a good, hard look at a school lunch? For many adults, it's probably been years—decades even—since they last thought about students' midday meals. If they did stop to ponder, they might picture something reasonably wholesome if not very exciting: a peanut butter and jelly sandwich paired with an apple, or a traditional plate of meat, potatoes and veggies. At worst, they may think, kids are making due with some pizza and a carton of milk.

The truth, though, is that many students aren't even getting the meager nutrients offered up by a simple slice of pizza. Instead, schools are serving up heaping helpings of previously frozen, recently fried delicacies like french fries and chicken nuggets. These high-carb, low-protein options are usually paired with a limp, flavorless, straight-from-the-freezer vegetable that quickly gets tossed in the trash. And that carton of milk? It's probably a sugar-filled chocolate sludge, or it's been replaced with a student's favorite high-calorie soda.

So what, you might ask. Kids like to eat junk food—it's a habit they'll grow out of soon enough. Besides, parents can always pack lunches for students looking for something better. But is that really the lesson we want to be teaching our kids? Many of those children aren't going to grow out of bad habits; they're going to reach adulthood thinking that ketchup is a vegetable. And students in low-income families are particularly impacted by the sad state of school food. These parents rely on schools to provide a warm, nutritious meal because they don't have the time or money to prepare food at home. Do we really want to be punishing these children with soggy meat patties and salt-soaked potato chips?

1. Both authors are arguing for the important of improving childhood nutrition. How do the authors' strategies differ?

A) Passage 1 presents several competing viewpoints while Passage 2 offers a single argument.

B) Passage 1 uses scientific data while Passage 2 uses figurative language.

C) Passage 1 is descriptive while Passage 2 uses a cause-effect structure.

D) Passage 1 is friendly in tone while Passage 2 is angry.

The first author uses scientific facts (*the Centers for Disease Control found...* and *Even this small amount of exercise has been proven...*) to back up his argument, while the second uses figurative language (the ironic *delicacies* and the metaphor *sugar-filled chocolate sludge*), so **the correct answer is B)**. Answer A) is incorrect because the first author does present any opposing viewpoints. Answer C) is incorrect because Passage 2 does not have a cause-effect structure. And while the author of the second passage could be described as angry, the first author is not particularly friendly, so you can eliminate answer D) as well.

2. Both authors argue that—

    A) children should learn healthy eating habits at a young age.

    B) low-income students are disproportionately affected by the low-quality food offered in schools.

    C) teaching children about good nutrition will lower their chances of developing diabetes as adults.

    D) schools should provide children an opportunity to exercise every day.

Both authors argue children should learn healthy eating habits at a young age (answer A). The author of Passage 1 states that *a child who grows up living an unhealthy lifestyle is likely to become an adult who does the same*, and the author of Passage 2 states that *many of those children aren't going to grow out of bad habits*—both of these sentences argue that it's necessary to teach children about nutrition early in life. Answers C) and D) are mentioned only by the author of Passage 1, and answer B) is only discussed in Passage 2.

3

WRITING

The PERT will consider five aspects of writing: focus, or how clearly you maintain your stance on the issue; organization, or your ability to clearly structure your essay and ideas; development and support, or your ability to develop your argument and present examples strengthening it; sentence structure, including correct and varied sentence construction; and mechanical conventions, including correct use of grammar and punctuation. You won't actually be writing an essay, but you still need to know writing rules to answer questions about texts. A review of essential writing skills follows below.

WRITING STRUCTURE

There are many ways to organize a body of text, and there are a few main things you can do to ensure that whatever structure you choose will work.

The first thing to realize is that there are many different kinds of texts. Each one has slightly different methods of delivering an idea, but they all have the same basic parts—introduction, body, and conclusion. The most common texts are persuasive and expository. A persuasive text takes a position on an issue and attempts to show the reader why it is correct. An expository text explains different aspects of an issue without necessarily taking a side. Each of these essay types can be developed using various different methods.

Introductions

Use an introduction and a conclusion that frame the argument or idea. The introduction is a good place to bring up complexities, counterarguments, and context, all things that will help the reader understand why you chose the response you did. In the conclusion, revisit those issues and wrap all of them up.

Below is an example of an introduction for one of the thesis statements from the previous section. Note that it gives some context for the argument, acknowledges the opposite side, and gives the reader a good idea of what complexities the issue holds.

> Technology has changed massively in the last several years, but today's generation barely notices—high school students today are experienced with the internet, computers, apps, cameras, cell phones, and all kinds of technology. Teenagers need to be taught to use all these things safely and responsibly. Opponents of 1:1 technology programs might argue that students will be distracted or misuse the technology, but that is exactly why schools and teachers must teach them to use it. By providing technology to students, schools can help them use it for things such as creating great projects with other students, keeping in touch with teachers and classmates, and researching for class projects. In a world where technology is improving and changing at a phenomenal rate, schools have a responsibility to teach students how to navigate that technology safely and effectively, and providing each student with a laptop or tablet is one way to help them do that.

The Body Paragraphs

Group similar ideas together and have a plan for paragraphs. You don't want one big chunk of a paragraph. Some ways to organize your responses include creating paragraphs that describe or explain each reason given in the thesis; addressing the issue as a problem and offering a solution in a separate paragraph; telling a story that demonstrates the point (make sure to break it into paragraphs around related ideas); comparing and contrasting the merits of two opposing sides of the issue.

Make sure that each paragraph is consistent inside— that there are no extra ideas that seem unrelated to the paragraph's main idea.

Example

(1) Providing students with their own laptop or tablet will allow them to explore new programs and software in class with teachers and classmates and then practice at home. (2) In schools without laptops for students, classes have to visit computer labs, where they share old, used up computers that often have the keys missing or run so slowly they can barely be turned on before class ends. (3) If a teacher tries to show students how to use a new tool or website, then students have to scramble to follow along and have no chance to explore the possibilities of the new tool. (4) If they have laptops to take home instead, students can do things like practice editing

video clips or photographs until they are perfect; they can email a classmate or use shared files to collaborate even after school. **(5)** The laptops have potential to be a distraction to the students and lead to lower academic performances. **(6)** If schools expect students to learn these skills, it is their responsibility to provide students enough opportunities to practice them.

Which sentence does NOT belong in this paragraph?

A) 1

B) 3

C) 4

D) 5

The sentence that doesn't belong is choice D) 5. While it is about the topic of the paragraph (students having laptops at school), it's not about the main idea of the paragraph, which is that students should have them.

Conclusions

In order to get the best ending, choose a conclusion that reminds the reader why you were talking about these topics in the first place. Go back to the ideas in the introduction and thesis sentence, but be careful not to simply restate ideas.

Here is a sample conclusion paragraph that could go with the previous introduction. Notice that this conclusion talks about the same topics as the introduction (changing technology and the responsibility of schools), but it does not simply rewrite the thesis.

> As technology continues to change, teens will continue to need to adapt to it. Schools already teach people how to interact and fit into society, so it makes sense that they would also teach how to fit technology into the equation of our lives. Providing students with their own devices is one step in that important task, and should be supported or encouraged in all schools.

WRITING A THESIS STATEMENT

The thesis, a key organizational tool in any text, tells readers specifically what you think and what you will say. Without a strong, direct thesis statement, readers have to deduce the main idea on their own.

Choosing a good thesis sentence really comes down to one thing: simply state the idea and why it is true or correct.

PROVIDING SUPPORTING EVIDENCE

Your responses not only needs structured, organized paragraphs, it also needs to provide specific supporting evidence for the argument.

Any time a general statement is made, it should be followed by specific evidence that will help to convince the reader that the argument has merit. The specific examples do not give new ideas to the paragraph; rather, they explain or defend the general ideas that have already been stated.

The following are some other examples of general statements and specific statements that provide more detailed support:

GENERAL: Students may get distracted online or access harmful websites.

SPECIFIC: Some students spend too much time using chat features or social media, or they get caught up in online games. Others spend time reading websites that have nothing to do with an assignment.

SPECIFIC: Teens often think they are hidden behind their computer screens. If teenagers give out personal information such as age or location on a website, it can lead to dangerous strangers seeking them out.

GENERAL: Many different types of animals can make good family pets.

SPECIFIC: Labrador Retrievers are friendly and enjoy spending time with the family, though it will be important to walk the dog often.

SPECIFIC: On the other hand, pets such as gerbils, mice, hamsters, or rats can be very affectionate and are much more contained—so it is easier to keep their living area clean.

WRITING WELL

Transitions

Transitions are words, sentences, and ideas that help connect one piece of writing to another. You should use them between sentences and between paragraphs. Some common transitions include then, next, in other words, as well, in addition to. Be creative with your transitions, if possible, and make sure you understand what the transition you are using shows about the relationship between the ideas. For instance, the transition although implies that there is some contradiction between the first idea and the second.

Syntax

The way you write sentences is important to maintaining the interest of a reader. Try to begin sentences differently. Make some sentences long and some sentences short. Write simple sentences. Write complex sentences that have complex ideas in them. Readers appreciate variety.

There are four basic types of sentences: simple, compound, complex, and compound-complex. Try to use some of each type. Be careful that the sentences make sense, though—it is better to have clear and simple writing that a reader can understand than to have complex, confusing syntax that does not clearly express the idea.

Word Choice and Tone

The words you choose influence the impression you make on readers. There are two important things you need to do. Firstly, use words that are specific, direct, and appropriate to the task—complex and impressive; simple and direct; or even neutral. Use the best words you know and do your best to avoid using vague, general words such as good, bad, very, or a lot. Words like these have unclear meanings from being used in many different situations —they can mean different things depending on the situation. Secondly, make sure that you actually use words you know! Trying to fit in too many "million-dollar words," may result in using some you do not know as well and thus use incorrectly; try to fit in words that you know make sense in the context.

PARTS OF SPEECH

Nouns and Pronouns

NOUNS are people, places, or things. They are typically the subject of a sentence. For example, in the sentence *The hospital was very clean*, the noun is hospital; it is a place. PRONOUNS replace nouns and make sentences sound less repetitive. Take the sentence *Sam stayed home from school because Sam was not feeling well*. The word Sam appears twice in the same sentence. Instead, you can use a pronoun and say *Sam stayed at home because he did not feel well*. Sounds much better, right?

Because pronouns take the place of nouns, they need to agree both in number and gender with the noun they replaced. So, a plural noun needs a plural pronoun, and a feminine noun needs a feminine pronoun. In the previous sentence, for example, the plural pronoun *they* replaced the plural noun pronouns.

> #### Examples
>
> Wrong: If a student forgets their homework, it is considered incomplete.
>
> Correct: If a student forgets his or her homework, it is considered incomplete.
>
> **Student is a singular noun, but their is a plural pronoun. So, this first sentence is grammatically incorrect. To correct it, replace their with the singular pronoun his or her.**
>
> Wrong: Everybody will receive their paychecks promptly.
>
> Correct: Everybody will receive his or her paycheck promptly.

SINGULAR PRONOUNS
- I, me, mine, my
- You, your, yours
- He, him, his
- She, her, hers
- It, its

PLURAL PRONOUNS
- We, us, our, ours
- They, them, their, theirs

Everybody is a singular noun, but their is a plural pronoun. So, this sentence is grammatically incorrect. To correct it, replace their with the singular pronoun his or her.

Wrong: When a nurse begins work at a hospital, you should wash your hands.

Correct: When a nurse begins work at a hospital, he or she should wash his or her hands.

This sentence begins in third-person perspective and finishes in second-person perspective. So, this sentence is grammatically incorrect. To correct it, ensure the sentence finishes with third-person perspective.

Wrong: After the teacher spoke to the student, she realized her mistake.

Correct: After Mr. White spoke to his student, she realized her mistake. (she and her referring to student)

Correct: After speaking to the student, the teacher realized her own mistake. (her referring to teacher)

This sentence refers to a teacher and a student. But who does she refer to, the teacher or the student? To improve clarity, use specific names or state more specifically who spotted the mistake.

Verbs

Remember the old commercial, "Verb: It's what you do"? That sums up verbs in a nutshell. A verb is the action of a sentence; verbs "do" things. Verb must be conjugated to match the context of the sentence; this can sometimes be tricky because English has many irregular verbs. For example, runs is an action verb in the present tense that becomes ran in the past tense; the linking verb is (which describes a state of being) becomes was in the past tense.

Think of the subject and the verb as sharing a single *s*. If the noun ends with an *s*, the noun shouldn't and vice versa.

Table 3.1. Conjugations of the verb *to be*

	PAST	PRESENT	FUTURE
SINGULAR	was	is	will be
PLURAL	were	are	will be

If the subject is separated from the verb, cross out the phrases between them to make conjugation easier.

As mentioned, verbs must use the correct tense, and that tense must make sense in the context of the sentence. For example, the sentence *I was baking cookies and eat some dough* sounds strange, right? That's because the two verbs *was baking* and *eat* are in different tenses. *Was baking* occurred in the past; *eat*, on the other hand, occurs in the present. Instead, it should be *ate some dough*.

Like pronouns, verbs must agree in number with the noun they refer back to. In the example above, the verb *was* refers back to the singular *I*. If the subject of the sentence was plural, it would need to be modified to read *They were baking cookies and ate some dough*.

Note that the verb *ate* does not change form; this is common for verbs in the past tense.

Examples

Wrong: The cat chase the ball while the dogs runs in the yard.

Correct: The cat chases the ball while the dogs run in the yard.

Cat is singular, so it takes a singular verb (which confusingly ends with an s); dogs is plural, so it needs a plural verb.

Wrong: The cars that had been recalled by the manufacturer was returned within a few months.

Correct: The cars that had been recalled by the manufacturer were returned within a few months.

Sometimes, the subject and verb are separated by clauses or phrases. Here, the subject cars is separated from the verb phrase were returned, making it more difficult to conjugate the verb.

Correct: The deer hid in the trees.

Correct: The deer are not all the same size.

The subject of these sentences is a collective noun, which describes a group of people or items. This noun can be singular if its referring to the group as a whole or plural if it refers to each item in the group as a separate entity.

Correct: The doctor and nurse work in the hospital.

Correct: Neither the nurse nor her boss was scheduled to take a vacation.

Correct: Either the patient or her parents need to sign the release forms.

When the subject contains two or more nouns connected by and, that subject is plural and requires a plural verb. Singular subjects joined by or, either/or, neither/nor, or not only/ but also remain singular; when these words join plural and singular subjects, the verb should match the closest subject.

Wrong: Because it will rain during the party last night, we had to move the tables inside.

Correct: Because it rained during the party last night, we had to move the tables inside.

All the verb tenses in a sentence need to agree both with each other and with the other information in the sentence. In the first sentence above, the tense doesn't match the other information in the sentence: last night indicates the past (rained) not the future (will rain).

Adjectives and Adverbs

Adjectives are words that describe a noun. Take the sentence The boy hit the ball. If you want to know more about the noun *boy*, then you could use an adjective to describe it: *The little boy hit the ball.* An adjective simply provides more information about a noun or subject in a sentence.

For some reason, many people have a difficult time with adverbs, but don't worry! They are really quite simple. Adverbs and adjectives are similar because they provide more information about a part of a sentence; however, they do not describe nouns—that's an adjective's job. Instead, adverbs describe verbs, adjectives, and even other adverbs. For example, in the sentence *The doctor had recently hired a new employee*, the adverb *recently* tells us more about how the action *hired* took place.

Adjectives, adverbs, and modifying phrases (groups of words that together modify another word) should always be placed as close as possible to the word they modify. Separating words from their modifiers can create incorrect or confusing sentences.

Examples

Wrong: Running through the hall, the bell rang and the student knew she was late.

Correct: Running through the hall, the student heard the bell ring and knew she was late.

The phrase running through the hall should be placed next to student, the noun it modifies.

Wrong: Of my two friends, Clara is the most smartest.

Correct: Of my two friends, Clara is more smart.

The first sentence above has two mistakes. First, the word most should only be used when comparing three or more things. Second, the adjective should only be modified with more/most or the suffix -er/-est, not both.

Other Parts of Speech

Prepositions express the location of a noun or pronoun in relation to other words and phrases in a sentence. For example, in the sentence *The nurse parked her car in a parking garage*, the preposition *in* describes the position of the car in relation to the garage. The noun that follows the preposition is called it's object. In the example above, the object of the preposition *in* is the noun *parking garage*.

Conjunctions connect words, phrases, and clauses. The conjunctions summarized in the acronym FANBOYS—*for, and, nor, but, or, yet, so*—are called coordinating conjunctions and are used to join independent clauses. For example, in the sentence *The nurse prepared the patient for surgery, and the doctor performed the surgery*, the conjunction *and* joins together the two independent clauses. Subordinating conjunctions like *although, because,* and *if* join together an independent and dependent

See *Phrases and Clauses* for more on independent and dependent clauses.

clause. In the sentence *She had to ride the subway because her car was broken*, the conjunction *because* joins together the two clauses.

Interjections, like *wow* and *hey*, express emotion and are most commonly used in conversation and casual writing.

Examples

Choose the word that best completes the sentence.

1. Her love _____ blueberry muffins kept her coming back to the bakery every week.

   A) to

   B) with

   C) of

   D) about

   The correct preposition is *of* (choice C).

2. Christine left her house early on Monday morning, _____ she was still late for work.

   A) but

   B) and

   C) for

   D) or

   In this sentence, the conjunction is joining together two contrasting ideas, so the correct answer is *but* (choice A).

CONSTRUCTING SENTENCES

Phrases and Clauses

A **PHRASE** is a group of words acting together that contain either a subject or verb, but not both. Phrases can be made from many different parts of speech. For example, a prepositional phrases includes a preposition and the object of that preposition (e.g., under the table), and a verb phrase includes the main verb and any helping verbs (e.g., had been running). Phrases cannot stand along as a sentence.

A **CLAUSE** is a group of words that contains both a subject and a verb. There are two types of clauses: independent clauses can stand alone as a sentence, and dependent clauses cannot stand alone. Dependent clauses begin with a subordinating conjunction.

Examples

Classify each of the following as a phrase, independent clause, or dependent clause:

   1. I have always wanted to drive a bright red sports car

   2. under the bright sky filled with stars

   3. because my sister is running late

Number 1 is an independent clause—it has a subject (I) and a verb (have wanted) and has no subordinating conjunction. Number 2 is a phrase made up of a preposition (under), its object (sky), and words that modify sky (bright, filled with stars). Number 3 is a dependent clause—it has a subject (sister), a verb (is running), and a subordinating conjunction (because).

Types of Sentences

A sentence can be classified as simple, compound, complex, or compound-complex based on the type and number of clauses it has.

Table 3.2. Types of sentences

SENTENCE TYPE	NUMBER OF INDEPENDENT CLAUSES	NUMBER OF DEPENDENT CLAUSES
simple	one	zero
compound	two or more	zero
complex	one	one or more
compound-complex	two or more	one or more

A SIMPLE SENTENCE consists of only one independent clause. Because there are no dependent clauses in a simple sentence, it can simply be a two-word sentence, with one word being the subject and the other word being the verb (e.g., I ran.). However, a simple sentence can also contain prepositions, adjectives, and adverbs. Even though these additions can extend the length of a simple sentence, it is still considered a simple sentence as long as it doesn't contain any dependent clauses.

COMPOUND SENTENCES have two or more independent clauses and no dependent clauses. Usually a comma and a coordinating conjunction (and, or, but, nor, for, so, and yet) join the independent clauses, though semicolons can be used as well. For example, the sentence My computer broke, so I took it to be repaired is compound.

COMPLEX SENTENCES have one independent clause and at least one dependent clause. In the complex sentence If you lie down with dogs, you'll wake up with fleas, the first clause is dependent (because of the subordinating conjunction if), and the second is independent.

COMPOUND-COMPLEX SENTENCES have two or more independent clauses and at least one subordinate clause. For example, the sentence Even though David was a vegetarian, he went with his friends to steakhouses, but he focused on the conversation instead of the food, is compound-complex.

Examples

Classify: San Francisco in the springtime is one of my favorite places to visit.

Although the sentence is lengthy, it is simple because it contains only one subject and verb (San Francisco... is) modified by additional phrases.

Classify: I love listening to the radio in the car because I can sing along as loud as I want.

The sentence has one independent clause (I love . . . car) and one dependent (because I . . . want), so it's complex.

Classify: I wanted to get a dog, but I have a fish because my roommate is allergic to pet dander.

This sentence has three clauses: two independent (I wanted . . . dog and I have a fish) and one dependent (because my . . . dander), so it's compound-complex.

Classify: The game was cancelled, but we will still practice on Saturday.

This sentence is made up of two independent clauses joined by a conjunction (but), so it's compound.

Clause Placement

In addition to the classifications above, sentences can also be defined by the location of the main clause. In a periodic sentence, the main idea of the sentence is held until the end. In a cumulative sentence, the independent clause comes first, and any modifying words or clauses follow it. Note that this type of classification—periodic or cumulative—is not used in place of the simple, compound, complex, or compound-complex classifications. A sentence can be both cumulative and complex, for example.

Examples

Classify: To believe your own thought, to believe that what is true for you in your private heart is true for all men, that is genius.

In this sentence the main independent clause—that is genius—is held until the very end, so it's periodic. It's also simple because it has one independent clause.

Classify: We need the tonic of wildness—to wade sometimes in marshes where the bittern and meadow-hen lurk, and hear the booming of the snipe; to smell the whispering sedge where only some wilder and more solitary fowl builds her nest, and the mink crawls with its belly close to the ground.

Here, the main clause—we need the tonic of wildness—is at the beginning, so the sentence is cumulative. It's also simple because it has one main clause.

PUNCTUATION

The basic rules for using the major punctuation marks are given in the following table.

Table 3.3. How to use punctuation

PUNCTUATION	USED FOR	EXAMPLE
period	ending sentences	Periods go at the end of complete sentences
question Mark	ending questions	What's the best way to end a sentence?
exclamation Point	ending sentences that show extreme emotion	I'll never understand how to use commas!
comma	joining two independent clauses (always with a coordinating conjunction)	Commas can be used to join clauses, but they must always be followed by a coordinating conjunction
	setting apart introductory and nonessential words and phrases	Commas, when used properly, set apart extra information in a sentence.
	separating items in a list	My favorite punctuation marks include the colon, semicolon, and period.
semicolon	joining together two independent clauses (never with a conjunction)	I love exclamation points; they make sentences so exciting!
Colon	introducing a list, explanation or definition	When I see a colon, I know what to expect: more information.
Apostrophe	form contractions	It's amazing how many people can't use apostrophes correctly.
	show possession	Parentheses are my sister's favorite punctuation; she finds commas' rules confusing.
Quotation Marks	indicate a direct quote	I said to her, "Tell me more about parentheses."

Examples

Wrong: Her roommate asked her to pick up milk, and watermelon from the grocery store.

Correct: Her roommate asked her to pick up milk and watermelon from the grocery store.

Commas are only needed when joining three items in a series; this sentence only has two (milk and watermelon).

Wrong: The coach of the softball team—who had been in the job for only a year, quit unexpectedly on Friday.

Correct: The coach of the softball team—who had been in the job for only a year—quit unexpectedly on Friday.

Correct: The coach of the softball team, who had been in the job for only a year, quit unexpectedly on Friday.

When setting apart nonessential words and phrases, you can use either dashes or commas, but not both.

Wrong: I'd like to order a hamburger, from my favorite restaurant, but my friend says I should get a sandwich instead.

Correct: I'd like to order a hamburger from my favorite restaurant, but my friend says I should get a sandwich instead.

Prepositional phrases are almost always essential to the sentences, meaning they don't need to be set apart with commas. Note that the second comma remains because it is separating two independent clauses.

CAPITALIZATION

- The first word of a sentence is always capitalized.
- The first letter of a proper nouns is always capitalized. (We're going to Chicago on Wednesday.)
- The first letter of an adjectives derived from a proper noun is capitalized. (The play was described by critics as Shakespearian.)
- Titles are capitalized if they precede the name they modify. (President Obama met with Joe Biden, his vice president.)
- Months are capitalized, but not the names of the seasons. (Snow fell in March even though winter was over.)
- School subjects are not capitalized unless they are themselves proper nouns. (I will have chemistry and French tests tomorrow.)

Example

Which sentence contains an error in capitalization?

A) She wrote many angry letters, but only senator Phillips responded to her request.

B) Matthew lives on Main Street and takes the bus to work every weekday.

C) Maria's goal has always wanted to be an astronaut, so she's studying astronomy in school.

D) Although his birthday is in February, Will decided to celebrate early by eating at Francisco's, his favorite restaurant.

POINT OF VIEW

A sentence's **POINT OF VIEW** is the perspective from which it is written. Point of view is described as either first, second, or third person.

Table 3.4. Point of view

PERSON	PRONOUNS USED	WHO'S ACTING?	EXAMPLE
first	I, we	The writer	I take my time when shopping for shoes.
second	you	The reader	You prefer to shop online.
third	he, she, it, they	The subject	She buys shoes from her cousin's store.

Using first person is best for writing in which the writer's personal experiences, feelings, and opinions are an important element. Second person is best for writing in which the author directly addresses the reader. Third person is most common in formal and academic writing; it creates distance between the writer and the reader. A sentence's point of view has to remain consistent throughout the sentence.

Look for pronouns to help you identify which point of view a sentence is using.

Example

Wrong: If someone wants to be a professional athlete, you have to practice often.

Correct: If you want to be a professional athlete, you have to practice often.

Correct: If someone wants to be a professional athlete, he or she has to practice often.

In the first sentence, the person shifts from third (someone) to second *(you)*. It needs to be rewritten to be consistent.

ACTIVE AND PASSIVE VOICE

Sentences can be written in active voice or passive voice. **ACTIVE VOICE** means that the subjects of the sentences are performing the action of the sentence. In a sentence in **PASSIVE VOICE**, the subjects are being acted on. So, the sentence *Justin wrecked my car* is in the active voice because the subject (*Justin*) is doing the action (*wrecked*). The sentence can be rewritten in passive voice by using a *to be* verb: *My car was wrecked by Justin*. Now the subject of the sentence (*car*) is being acted on. Notice that it's possible to write the sentence so that the person performing the action is not identified: *My car was wrecked*.

Generally, good writing will make more use of the active than passive voice. However, passive voice can sometimes be the better choice. For example, if it's not known who or what performed the action of the sentence, it's necessary to use passive voice.

Examples

Rewrite the following sentence in active voice: *I was hit with a stick by my brother.*

To rewrite a sentence in active voice, first take the person or object performing the action (usually given in a prepositional phrase) and make it the subject. Then, the subject of the original sentence becomes the object and the *to be* verb disappears: **My brother hit me with a stick.**

Rewrite the following sentence in passive voice: *My roommate made coffee this morning.*

To rewrite a sentence in passive voice, the object (*coffee*) becomes the subject, and the subject gets moved to a prepositional phrase at the end of the sentence. Lastly, the *to be* verb is added: **The coffee was made this morning by my roommate.**

TRANSITIONS

Transitions join together two ideas and also explain the logical relationship between those ideas. For example, the transition *because* tells you that two things have a cause and effect relationship, while the transitional phrase *on the other hand* introduces a contradictory idea. On the PERT Writing section, you will definitely need to make good use of transitions.

Table 3.5. Common transition words

CAUSE AND EFFECT	as a result, because, consequently, due to, if/then, so, therefore, thus
SIMILARITY	also, likewise, similarly
CONTRAST	but, however, in contrast, on the other hand, nevertheless, on the contrary, yet
CONCLUDING	briefly, finally, in conclusion, in summary, thus, to, conclude
ADDITION	additionally, also, as well, further, furthermore, in addition, moreover
EXAMPLES	in other words, for example, for instance, to illustrate
TIME	after, before, currently, later, recently, since, subsequently, then, while

CONTINUE

Examples

Choose the transition that would best fit in the blank.

1. Clara's car breaks down frequently. _____, she decided to buy a new one.

2. Chad scored more points than any other player on his team. _____, he is often late to practice, so his coach won't let him play in the game Saturday.

3. Miguel will often his lunch outside. _____, on Wednesday he took his sandwich to the park across from his office.

4. Alex set the table _____ the lasagna finished baking in the oven.

   A) however

   B) for example

   C) while

   D) therefore

Sentence 1 is describing a cause (her car breaks down) and an effect (she'll buy a new one), so the correct transition is *therefore*. **Sentence 2 includes a contrast: it would make sense for Chad to play in the game, but he isn't, so the best transition is** *however*. **In Sentence 3, the clause after the transition is an example, so the best transition is** *for example*. **In Sentence 4, two things are occurring at the same time, so the best transition is** *while*.

HOMOPHONES AND SPELLING

The PERT will include questions that ask you to identify the correct **HOMOPHONE**, which is a set of words that are pronounced similarly but have different meanings. Bawl and ball, for example, are homophones. You will also be tested on spelling, so it's good to familiarize yourself with commonly misspelled words.

COMMON HOMOPHONES
- Bare/bear
- Brake/break
- Die/dye
- Effect/affect
- Flour/flower
- Heal/heel
- Insure/ensure
- Morning/mourning
- Peace/piece
- Poor/pour
- Principal/principle
- Sole/soul
- Stair/stare
- Suite/sweet
- Their/there/they're
- Wear/where

Examples

Choose the sentence that contains the correct spelling of the underlined word.

1. Her excellent manors and friendly personality made it easy for her to win new clients.

2. Her excellent manners and friendly personality made it easy for her to win new clients.

3. Her excellent manors and friendly personality maid it easy for her to win new clients.

4. Her excellent manners and friendly personality maid it easy for her to win new clients.

People's behavior towards others are *manners*, while a *manor* is a country house. A *maid* is a person who cleans and *made* is the past tense of make. **So, the correct answer is 2.**

1. The nurse has three patents to see before lunch.
2. The nurse has three patience to see before lunch.
3. The nurse has three patients to see before lunch.
4. The nurse has three pateince to see before lunch.

The correct spelling of *patients* is found in answer choice 3.

PRACTICE TEST

MATHEMATICS

1. What is the value of the expression $\frac{x^2 - 2y}{y}$ when $x = 20$ and $y = \frac{x}{2}$?

A) 0

B) 19

C) 36

D) 38

2. $3x^3 + 4x - (2x + 5y) + y =$

A) $11x - 4y$

B) $29x - 4y$

C) $3x^3 + 2x - 4y$

D) $3x^3 + 2x + y$

3. If $10y - 8 - 2y = 4y - 22 + 5y$, then $y =$?

A) -30

B) $-4\frac{2}{3}$

C) 14

D) 30

4. Which of the following lists of numbers is in order from least to greatest?

A) $\frac{1}{7}, 0.125, \frac{6}{9}, 0.60$

B) $\frac{1}{7}, 0.125, 0.60, \frac{6}{9}$

C) $0.125, \frac{1}{7}, 0.60, \frac{6}{9}$

D) $\frac{1}{7}, 0.125, \frac{6}{9}, 0.60$

5. Which of the following expressions is equivalent to $6x + 5 \geq -15 + 8x$?

A) $x \leq -5$

B) $x \leq 5$

C) $x \leq 10$

D) $x \leq 20$

6. Jane earns $15 per hour babysitting. If she starts out with $275 in her bank account, which of the following equations represents how many hours (h) she will have to babysit for her account to reach $400?

A) $400 = 275 + 15h$

B) $400 = 15h$

C) $400 = \frac{15}{h} + 275$

D) $400 = -275 - 15h$

7. At a bake sale, muffins are priced at $1.50 each and cookies are priced at $1 for two. If 11 muffins are sold, and the total money earned is $29.50, how many cookies were sold?

A) 12

B) 13

C) 23

D) 26

8. If $(2x + 6)(3x - 15) = 0$, then $x =$?

A) $\{-5, 3\}$

B) $\{-3, 5\}$

C) $\{-2, -3\}$

D) $\{-6, 15\}$

9. Adam is painting the outside of a 4-walled shed. The shed is 5 feet wide, 4 feet deep, and 7 feet high. How many square feet of paint will Adam need?

A) 46

B) 63

C) 126

D) 140

10. $4x + 3y = 10$

$2x - y = 20$

How many solutions (x, y) are there to the system of equations above?

A) 0

B) 1

C) 2

D) more than 2

11. $\frac{-6 + 11}{2(-3 - 8)} =$

A) $-\frac{5}{22}$

B) $-\frac{1}{2}$

C) $\frac{5}{22}$

D) $\frac{5}{9}$

12. $64 - 100x^2 =$

A) $(8 + 10x)(8 - 10x)$

B) $(8 + 10x)(8x + 10)$

C) $(8 - 10x)^2$

D) $(8 + 10x)^2$

13. The graph of which of the following equations is a straight line parallel to the graph of $3y - 1 = 2x$?

A) $-3x + 2y = -2$

B) $-2x + 3y = 6$

C) $-2x + 2y = 3$

D) $-x + 3y = -2$

14. If $16x^2 + 8x + 1 = 0$, then $x^3 =$?

A) $-\frac{1}{16}$

B) $-\frac{1}{64}$

C) 1

D) 16

15. If $f(x) = x^2 + 3$ and $g(x) = 3x - 12$, then $f(g(5)) =$?

A) 12

B) 28

C) 32

D) 72

16. What is an x-intercept of the graph $y = x^2 - 7x + 12$?

A) -4

B) 0

C) 3

D) 7

17. The sequence $\{a_n\}$ is defined by $a_1 = 5$ and $a_{n+1} = a_n + 7$ for $n = 1, 2, 3,\ldots$ What is the value of a_5?

A) 12

B) 20

C) 26

D) 33

18. What is the value of the expression $0.5^x + 1$ when $x = -2$?

A) 0.75

B) 1.25

C) 5

D) 4

19. Which of the following equations represents a line that passes through the points (2, 7) and (6, 10)?

A) $y = -\frac{3}{4}x + 5\frac{1}{2}$

B) $y = -1\frac{1}{3}x - 4\frac{1}{2}$

C) $y = \frac{3}{4}x + 5\frac{1}{2}$

D) $y = \frac{4}{5}x - 5\frac{1}{2}$

20. What is the value of the expression $|3x - y| + |2y - x|$ if $x = -4$ and $y = -1$?

A) −13

B) −11

C) 11

D) 13

21. 11, 7, 3, −1,...

If 11 is defined as the first term in the sequence given above, which of the following functions describes the sequence?

A) $f(n) = 11 + 4(n - 1)$

B) $f(n) = 11(4)^{(n-1)}$

C) $f(n) = 11 - 4n$

D) $f(n) = 15 - 4n$

22. $m = 5^{-a}$

$m = 4^{-b}$

$m = 3^{-c}$

$m = 2^{-d}$

The variables a, b, c, and d each represent positive real numbers between 0 and 1. If m is a constant, which of the following expressions is true?

A) $a > b > c > d$

B) $b > a > c > d$

C) $c > d > b > a$

D) $d > c > b > a$

23. $\dfrac{(x^a y^b)(z^b y^a)}{z(xy)^a} =$

A) $y^b z^{(b-1)}$

B) $xy^b z^{(b-1)}$

C) $xy^{ab}z$

D) $\dfrac{y^b}{z^b}$

24. If $y = \log_3 x$, what is the value of y when $x = 81$?

A) 2

B) 4

C) 9

D) 27

25. As shown below, 2 identical circles are drawn next to each other with their sides just touching; both circles are enclosed in a rectangle whose sides are tangent to the circles. If each circle's radius is 2 inches, find the area of the rectangle.

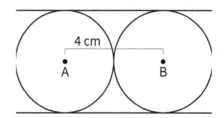

A) 8 cm²

B) 16 cm²

C) 24 cm²

D) 32 cm²

26. The county is instituting a new license plate system. The new plates will have 6 digits: the first digit will be 1, 2 or 3, and the next 5 digits can be any number from 0 – 9. How many possible unique combinations does this new system offer?

A) 53

B) 60

C) 3×10^5

D) 1×10^6

27. John and Jake are working at a car wash. It takes John 1 hour to wash 3 cars; Jake can wash 3 cars in 45 minutes. If they work together, how many cars can they wash in 1 hour?

A) 6

B) 7

C) 9

D) 12

28. Let $f(x) = 2x + 1$. If $g(x)$ is obtained by reflecting $f(x)$ across the y-axis and translating it 4 units in the positive y direction, what is $g(x)$?

A) $g(x) = -2x + 3$

B) $g(x) = -2x + 5$

C) $g(x) = 2x + 5$

D) $g(x) = 8x + 1$

29. The points $(-1, -1)$, $(-3, -8)$, $(0, 6)$ and $(5, 11)$ are plotted on a coordinate plane. How many of these 4 points are collinear with the points $(0, 1)$ and $(2, 5)$?

A) 0

B) 1

C) 2

D) 3

30. A plane makes a trip of 246 miles. For some amount of time, the plane's speed is 115 miles per hour. For the remainder of the trip, the plane's speed is 250 miles per hour. If the total trip time is 72 minutes, how many minutes did the plane fly at 115 miles per hour?

A) 18

B) 23

C) 24

D) 28

READING

Read each passage carefully, and answer the questions that follow.

Snakes

Skin coloration and markings have an important role to play in the world of snakes. Those intricate diamonds, stripes, and swirls help animals hide from predators and advertise to mates. Perhaps most importantly (for us humans, anyway), the markings can also indicate whether the snake is venomous. While it might seem counterintuitive for a poisonous snake to stand out in bright red or blue, that fancy costume tells any approaching predator that eating him would be a bad idea.

If you see a flashy looking snake out the woods, though, those marking don't necessarily mean it's poisonous: some snakes have a found a way to ward off predators without the actual venom. The California Kingsnake, for example, has very similar markings to the venomous Coral snake with whom it frequently shares a habitat. However, the Kingsnake is actually nonvenomous; it's merely pretending to be dangerous to eat. The Kingsnake itself eats lizards, rodents, birds, and even other snakes. A predatory hawk or eagle, usually hunting from high in the sky, can't tell the difference between the two species, and so the Kingsnake gets passed over and lives another day.

1. The writer's main purpose in the passage is to:

   A) explain how the markings on a snake are related to whether it is venomous.

   B) teach readers the difference between Coral snakes and Kingsnakes.

   C) illustrate why snakes are dangerous.

   D) demonstrate how animals survive in difficult environments.

2. Based on information contained in the passage, it is reasonable to infer that

   A) The Kingsnake is dangerous to humans.

   B) The Coral snake and the Kingsnake are both hunted by the same predators.

   C) It's safe to handle snakes in the woods because you can easily tell whether they're poisonous.

   D) The Kingsnake changes its marking when hawks or eagles are close by.

3. Which of the following statements best expresses the central idea of the passage?

   A) Humans can use coloration and markings on snakes to determine whether they're poisonous.

   B) Animals often use coloration and markings to attract mates and warn predators that they're poisonous.

   C) The California Kingsnake and Coral snake have nearly identical markings.

   D) Venomous snakes often have bright markings, although nonvenomous snakes can also mimic those colors.

4. Which sentence is least relevant to the main idea of the main idea of the passage?

   A) Perhaps most importantly (for us humans, anyway), the markings can also indicate whether the snake is venomous.

   B) The Kingsnake itself eats lizards, rodents, birds, and even other snakes.

   C) However, the Kingsnake is actually nonvenomous; it's merely pretending to be dangerous to eat.

   D) Skin coloration and markings have an important role to play in the world of snakes.

5. Which of the following is the best meaning of the word *intricate* as it is used in the first paragraph of the passage?

   A) natural

   B) colorful

   C) purposeful

   D) complicated

6. According to the passage, what is the difference between Kingsnakes and Coral snakes?

   A) Both Kingsnakes and Coral snakes are nonvenomous, but Coral snakes have colorful markings.

   B) Both Kingsnakes and Coral snakes are venomous, but Kingsnakes have colorful markings.

   C) Kingsnakes are nonvenomous while Coral snakes are venomous.

   D) Coral snakes are nonvenomous while Kingsnakes are venomous.

Hand Washing

Hand washing is one of our simplest and most powerful weapons against infection. The idea behind hand washing is deceptively simple. Many illnesses are spread when people touch infected surfaces, such as door handles or other people's hands, and then touch their own eyes, mouths, or noses. So, if pathogens can be removed from the hands before they spread, infections can be prevented. When done correctly, hand washing can prevent the spread of many dangerous bacteria and viruses, including those that cause the flu, the common cold, diarrhea, and many acute respiratory illnesses.

The most basic method of hand washing involves only soap and water. Just twenty seconds of scrubbing with soap and a complete rinsing with water is enough to kill and/or wash away many pathogens. The process doesn't even require warm water—studies have shown that cold water is just as effective at reducing the number of microbes on the hands. Antibacterial soaps are also available, although several studies have shown that simple soap and cold water is just as effective.

In recent years, hand sanitizers have become popular as an alternative to hand washing. These gels, liquids, and foams contain a high concentration of alcohol (usually at least 60 percent) which kills most bacteria and fungi; they can also be effective against some, but not all, viruses. There is a downside to hand sanitizer, however. Because the sanitizer isn't rinsed from hands, it only kills pathogens and does nothing to remove organic matter. So, hands "cleaned" with hand sanitizer may still harbor pathogens. Thus, while hand sanitizer can be helpful in situations where soap and clean water isn't available, a simple hand washing is still the best option.

7. Which of the following is the best meaning of the word *harbor* as it is used in the last paragraph of the passage?

   A) to disguise

   B) to hide

   C) to wash away

   D) to give a home

8. Which of the following best organizes the main topics addressed in this passage?

   A) I. Comparison of hand washing methods
   II. The disadvantages of hand sanitizer

   B) I. The importance of hand washing in preventing disease
   II. The benefits and problems with various methods of hand washing

   C) I. The relationship between hand washing and disease prevention
   II. Comparison of regular and anti-bacterial soaps

   D) I. How to effectively wash hands using soap and water
   II. How to clean hands using hand sanitizer

9. Which sentence, if inserted into the blank line in the sentence below, would be most consistent with the pattern of logic developed in the passage?

   Knowing that the temperature of the water does not affect the effectiveness of hand washing, it can be concluded that water plays an important role in hand washing because it

   _____

   A) has antibacterial properties

   B) physically removes pathogens from hands

   C) cools hands to make them inhospitable for dangerous bacteria

   D) is hot enough to kill bacteria

10. The writer's main purpose in the passage is to:

    A) persuade readers of the importance and effectiveness of hand washing with soap and cold water.

    B) dissuade readers from using hand sanitizer.

    C) explain how many common diseases are spread.

    D) describe the health benefits provided by hand washing and hand sanitizer.

11. Information presented in the passage best supports which of the following conclusions?

   A) Hand washing would do little to limit infections that spread through particles in the air.

   B) Hand washing is not necessary for people who do not touch their eyes, mouths, or noses with their hands.

   C) Hand sanitizer serves no purpose and should not be used as an alternative to hand washing.

   D) Hand sanitizer will likely soon replace hand washing as the preferred method of removing pathogens from hands.

12. Which of the following is not a fact stated in the passage?

   A) Many infections occur because people get pathogens on their hands and then touch their own eyes, mouths, or noses.

   B) Cold water is just as effective at removing pathogens as warm water.

   C) Antibacterial soaps and warm water are the best way to remove pathogens from hands.

   D) Hand sanitizer can be an acceptable alternative to hand washing when soap and water aren't available.

The Civil War

It could be said that the great battle between the North and South we call the Civil War was a battle for individual identity. The states of the South had their own culture, one based on farming, independence, and the rights of both man and state to determine their own paths. Similarly, the North had forged its own identity as a center of centralized commerce and manufacturing. This clash of lifestyles was bound to create tension, and this tension was bound to lead to war. But people who try to sell you this narrative are wrong. The Civil War was a not a battle of cultural identities—it was a battle about slavery. All other explanations for the war are either a direct consequence of the South's desire for wealth at the expense of her fellow man or a fanciful invention to cover up this sad portion of our nation's history. And it cannot be denied that this time in our past was very sad indeed. By denying our history, we make it even sadder.

13. The writer's main purpose in the passage is to:

   A) convince readers that slavery was the main cause of the Civil War.

   B) illustrate the cultural differences between the North and the South before the Civil War

   C) persuade readers that the North deserved to win the Civil War

   D) demonstrate that the history of the Civil War is too complicated to be understood clearly

14. Which of the following statements best expresses the central idea of the passage?

   A) The Civil War was the result of cultural differences between the North and South.

   B) The Civil War was caused by the South's reliance on slave labor.

   C) The North's use of commerce and manufacturing allowed it to win the war.

   D) The South's belief in the rights of man and state cost them the war.

15. Which of the following sentences from the passage best expresses a fact rather than an opinion?

   A) By denying our history, we make it even sadder.

   B) The states of the South had their own culture, one based on farming, independence, and the rights of both man and state to determine their own paths.

   C) The Civil War was a not a battle of cultural identities—it was a battle about slavery.

   D) And it cannot be denied that this time in our past is very sad indeed.

CONTINUE

16. Which of the following indicates how the author would likely state his position on the Civil War?

A) The Civil War was the result of cultural differences between the North and South.

B) The Civil War was caused by the South's reliance on slave labor.

C) The North's use of commerce and manufacturing allowed it to win the war.

D) The South's belief in the rights of man and state cost them the war.

17. Which of the following is the best meaning of the word *fanciful* as it is used in the passage?

A) complicated

B) imaginative

C) successful

D) unfortunate

Mason

Mason was one of those guys who just always seemed at home. Stick him on bus, and he'd make three new friends; when he joined a team, it was only a matter of time before he was elected captain. This particular skill rested almost entirely in his eyes. These brown orbs seemed lit from within, and when Mason focused that fire, it was impossible not to feel its warmth. People sought out Mason for the feeling of comfort he so easily created, and anyone with a good joke would want to tell it to Mason. His laughter started with a spark in his eyes that traveled down to create his wide, open smile.

18. Which of the following statements best expresses the central idea of the passage?

A) Mason was one of those guys who just always seemed at home.

B) Stick him on bus, and he'd make three new friends; when he joined a team, it was only a matter of time before he was elected captain.

C) These brown orbs seemed lit from within, and when Mason focused that fire, it was impossible not to feel its warmth.

D) People sought out Mason for the feeling of comfort he so easily created, and anyone with a good joke would want to tell it to Mason.

19. Based on information contained in the passage, it is reasonable to infer that

A) Mason has many friends.

B) Mason is very good at sports.

C) Mason does not like when strangers approach him.

D) Mason does not laugh often.

Temperature

Taking a person's temperature is one of the most basic and common health care tasks. Everyone from nurses to emergency medical technicians to concerned parents has needed to grab a thermometer and take somebody's temperature. But what's the best way to get an accurate reading? The answer depends on the situation.

The most common way people measure body temperature is orally. A simple digital or disposable thermometer is placed under the tongue for a few minutes, and the task is done. There are many situations, however, when measuring temperature orally isn't an option. For example, when a person can't breathe through his nose, he won't be able to keep his mouths closed long enough to get an accurate reading. In these situations, it's often preferable to place the thermometer in the rectum or armpit. Using the rectum also has the added benefit of providing a much more accurate reading than other locations can provide.

It's also often the case that certain people, like agitated patients or fussy babies, won't be able to sit still long enough for an accurate reading. In this situations, it's best to use a thermometer that works much more quickly, such as one that measures temperature in the ear or at the temporal artery. No matter which method is chosen, however, it's important to check the average temperature for the chosen region, as these can vary by several degrees.

20. The writer's main purpose in the passage is to:

A) advocate for the use of thermometers that measure temperature in the ear or at the temporal artery.

B) explain the methods available to measure a person's temperature and the situation where each method is appropriate.

C) warn readers that the average temperature of the human body varies by region.

D) discuss how nurses use different types of thermometers depending on the type of patient they are examining.

21. Which of the following statements best expresses the central idea of the passage?

A) It's important that everyone know the best way to take a person's temperature in any given situation.

B) The most common method of taking a person's temperature—orally—isn't appropriate is some situations.

C) The most accurate way to take a temperature is placing a digital thermometer in the rectum.

D) There are many different ways to take a person's temperature, and which is appropriate will depend on the situation.

22. Which of the following is the best meaning of the word *agitated* as it is used in the last paragraph of the passage?

A) obviously upset

B) quickly moving

C) violently ill

D) slightly dirty

23. According to the passage, why is it sometimes preferable to take a person's temperature rectally?

A) Rectal readings are more accurate than oral readings.

B) Many people cannot sit still long enough to have their temperatures taken orally.

C) Temperature readings can vary widely between regions of the body.

D) Many people do not have access to quick-acting thermometers.

24. Which of the following assumptions most influenced the writer's argument in the passage?

A) Getting an accurate temperature reading is an important part of basic medical care.

B) Nurses take patients' temperature more often than doctors.

C) Oral thermometers are the most commonly available and easy to use thermometer.

D) People who do not work in health care do not need to take temperatures often.

25. Which statement is not a fact from the passage?

A) Taking a temperature in the ear or at the temporal artery is more accurate than taking it orally.

B) If an individual cannot breathe through his nose, taking his temperature orally will likely give an inaccurate reading.

C) The standard human body temperature varies depending on whether it's measured in the mouth, rectum, armpit, ear, or temporal artery.

D) The most common way to measure temperature is by placing a thermometer in the mouth.

→

CONTINUE

Symbiosis

The bacteria, fungi, insects, plants, and animals that live together in a habitat have evolved to share a pool of limited resources. They've competed for water, minerals, nutrients, sunlight, and space, sometimes for thousands or even millions of years. As these communities have evolved, the species in them have developed complex, long-term interspecies interactions known as symbiotic relationships.

Ecologists characterize these interactions based on whether each party benefits. In mutualism both individuals benefit, while in synnecrosis both organisms are harmed. A relationship where one individual benefits and the other is harmed is known as parasitism. Examples of these relationships can easily be seen in any ecosystem. Pollination, for example, is mutualistic—pollinators get nutrients from the flower, and the plant is able to reproduce—while tapeworms, which steal nutrients from their host, are parasitic.

There's yet another class of symbiosis that is controversial among scientists. As it's long been defined, commensalism is a relationship where one species benefits and the other is unaffected. But is it possible for two species to interact and for one to remain completely unaffected? Often, relationships described as commensal include one species that feeds on another species' leftovers; remoras, for instance, will attach themselves to sharks and eat the food particles they leave behind. It might seem like the shark gets nothing from the relationship, but a closer look will show that sharks in fact benefit from remoras, which clean the sharks' skin and remove parasites. In fact, many scientists claim that relationships currently described as consensual are just mutualistic or parasitic in ways that haven't been discovered yet. Given the forces of natural selection that shape these relationships, it seems likely that they'll be proven right one day.

26. The writer's main purpose in the passage is to:

- **A)** argue that commensalism isn't actually found in nature.
- **B)** describe the many types of symbiotic relationships.
- **C)** explain how competition for resources results in long-term interspecies relationships.
- **D)** provide examples of the many different types of interspecies interactions.

27. Which of the following is the best meaning of the word *controversial* as it is used in the second paragraph of the passage?

- **A)** ignored
- **B)** hated
- **C)** confused
- **D)** debated

28. Why is commensalism controversial among scientists?

- **A)** Many scientists believe that an interspecies interaction where one species is unaffected does not exist.
- **B)** Some scientists believe that relationships where one species feeds on the leftovers of another should be classified as parasitism.
- **C)** Because remoras and sharks have a mutualistic relationship, no interactions should be classified as commensalism.
- **D)** Only relationships among animal species should be classified as commensalism.

29. Based on information contained in the passage, it is reasonable to infer what about symbiotic relationships?

- **A)** Scientists cannot decide how to classify symbiotic relationships among species.
- **B)** The majority of interspecies interactions are parasitic because most species do not get along.
- **C)** If two species are involved in a parasitic relationship, one of the species will eventually become extinct.
- **D)** Symbiotic relationships evolve as the species that live in a community adapt to their environments and each other.

30. Which of the following sentences in the passage best expresses an opinion rather than a fact?

A) Ecologists characterize these interactions based on whether each party benefits.

B) A relationship where one individual benefits and the other is harmed is known as parasitism.

C) There's yet another class of symbiosis that is controversial among scientists.

D) Given the forces of natural selection that shape these relationships, it seems likely that they'll be proven right one day.

WRITING

Read the passage below and answer the questions that follow.

Internet Cats

Who doesn't love a good cat meme? (1) It turns out that cats are more popular around the world than anyone had realized; with the proliferation of YouTube and social media, cats have taken the internet by storm. (2) From Grumpy Cat to Waffles, from the United States to Japan, cats appear in funny pictures, hilarious videos, and have even gone on to make their owners millions of dollars. (3)

Until recently, it had been believed that dogs were the most popular pet in the United States, with cats lagging behind in second place. (4) Dogs, "man's best friend," can be trained to do certain tricks and tasks, can be fun workout companions who play Frisbee and fetch with their owners, and can even help protect property. (5) While cats may have their uses in pest control, they are often reluctant to work on command, and very few are willing to submit to the humiliation of a collar and leash for a walk outside. (6) Still, it turns out that their funny antics and remarkable athletic prowess, even indoors, make for good TV.

(7) And so the internet is filled with cats large and small, lean and fat, wearing pieces of bread, making playthings out of boxes, jumping to amazing heights, and just looking hilariously grumpy. (8) Cats of internet fame now appear at conventions and festivals around the world, and people wait in line for hours just for a glimpse at their favorite feline celebrity. (9)

1. Which sentence best completes the first paragraph in order to create a good transition between two paragraphs?

A) But cats have not always been in the spotlight; in fact, they had been relegated to a secondary position in the known hierarchy of pet popularity in popular culture.

B) Indeed, cats are taking the world by storm.

C) Cats are by far the most popular pet in the world, and cat ownership continues to rise.

D) Thanks to the internet, cat marketability is becoming a field requiring true expertise, and there are even entrepreneurs who specialize in representing felines and their owners in public relations.

2. What would be a good title for this essay, keeping in mind both the topic and the tone?

A) The Rise and Fall of Famous Felines: From Grumpy Cat to Smushy Face

B) Canine versus Feline: the Battle Continues, from the Internet to the Convention Center

C) Felines Online! Pet Popularity, Feline Fame, and the Internet Age

D) Cats for Cash: is Feline Fame Really Catsploitation?

→

CONTINUE

3. Which of the following is the best revision of sentences (6) and (7)?

A) No change

B) Cats are useful for pest control, but they are often reluctant to work on command; moreover, very few are willing to submit to the humiliation of a collar and leash for a walk outside. (6) But it turns out that cats are more interesting – and funnier – than anyone realized, and their antics make for good TV. (7)

C) On the other hand, cats have their uses in pest control, they are often reluctant to work on command, and very few are willing to submit to the humiliation of a collar and leash for a walk outside. (6) However, it turns out that their funny antics and remarkable athletic prowess, even indoors, make for good TV. (7)

D) Cats are funnier and more interesting than dogs, but are only good for pest control – they won't go for walks on leashes or learn commands.

4. What would be the best sentence to follow sentence 9, in keeping with the theme of the entire paragraph?

A) We mourn internet sensations like Chairman Meow who have passed on, and laud newcomers like Smushy Face who have risen to the challenge of feline fame.

B) Some of the cat owners have become quite media savvy, and their cats now grace everything from coffee mugs to key chains to t-shirts; while waiting in line, fans are often enticed to buy these trinkets, but this irritates some fans.

C) Some dog owners are getting in on the act too, filming their dogs doing funny things and putting them on YouTube, but they don't get nearly as many hits as the cats do…at least not yet.

D) Some commentators believe that the cat owners are exploiting their cats, who no doubt would prefer to be at home napping in the sun or chasing mice.

5. Many people think that the U.S. president is elected directly by the people, but that is not exactly the case. Each candidate has a group of electors; these electors are members of the Electoral College. When Americans vote at the polls for the president, they are actually voting for their candidate's group of electors, who then technically vote in the president.

Which sentence best concludes the above paragraph?

A) So even though the people do ultimately choose the president, it is not in a direct election.

B) The Electoral College is really confusing.

C) Some Americans, however, believe that the Electoral College should be abolished.

D) Clearly, most people do not understand the presidential election.

6. Choose the word or words that best complete the sentence.

They left for the party, but Rebecca had to return home because _____ forgot her purse.

A) he

B) they

C) we

D) she

7. Choose the sentence that is written correctly.

A) Having finished her essay, washing the truck was the thing Maricela was ready to do.

B) Having finished her essay, Maricela had another thing she was ready to do and that was washing the truck.

C) Having finished her essay, washing the truck Maricela was ready to do.

D) Having finished her essay, Maricela was ready to wash the truck.

8. Choose the sentence that is written correctly.

   A) Hearing a lot on the news that pet ownership is beneficial to health, especially for those with high blood pressure.

   B) One often hears on the news that pet ownership is beneficial to health, especially for those with high blood pressure.

   C) The news hears a lot that pet ownership is beneficial to health, especially for those with high blood pressure.

   D) It is frequently heard in the news that pet ownership is beneficial to health, especially for those with high blood pressure.

9. Choose the word or words that best complete the sentence.

   During the 1950s, rock and roll music _____ very popular.

   A) become

   B) becoming

   C) became

   D) had became

10. Choose the word or words that best complete the sentence.

    Mai was _____ to her vacation.

    A) looking forward

    B) looking though

    C) looking at

    D) looking towards

11. Choose the sentence that is written correctly.

    A) Many consider television to be eroding of our nation's imaginations.

    B) Many consider television erosion of our nation's imaginations.

    C) Many consider television to erode our nation's imaginations.

    D) Many consider television to be eroding of the national imagination.

12. Choose the sentence that is written correctly.

    A) Does anyone have a guess that they would like to share before I reveal the answer?

    B) Is anyone having a guess that they would like to share before I reveal the answer?

    C) Do anyone have a guess that they would like to share before I reveal the answer?

    D) Anyone with a guess would like to share before I reveal the answer?

13. Choose the sentence that is grammatically correct.

    A) You can have either the cake nor the cookie.

    B) You can't have neither the cake or the cookie.

    C) You can have either the cake or the cookie.

    D) You can having either the cake or the cookie.

14. Choose the sentence that is written correctly.

    A) Raul, the most knowledgeable of us all, maintain that we would be needing better equipment.

    B) Raul, the most knowledgeable of us all, maintains that we would be needing better equipment.

    C) Raul, the most knowledgeable of us all, maintains that we would need better equipment.

    D) Raul, the most knowledgeable of us all, maintain we would have needed better equipment.

15. Choose the sentence that is written correctly.

    A) The meals at this restaurant have so much more salt in them than the restaurant we went to last week.

    B) The meals at this restaurant are so much saltier than the restaurant we went to last week.

    C) The meals at this restaurant have so much more salt in them than that other restaurant.

    D) The meals at this restaurant have so much more salt in them than those at the restaurant we went to last week.

16. Choose the sentence that is written correctly.

  A) Even though she knew it would reflect badly, the politician withdrawing her statement.

  B) Even though she knew it would reflect badly, the politician withdraws her statement.

  C) Even though she knew it would reflect badly, the politician was going to withdraw her statement.

  D) Even though she knew it would reflect badly, the politician withdrew her statement.

17. Choose the sentence that is written correctly.

  A) Tina and Marie had never seen anyone eating so loud.

  B) Tina and Marie had never seen anyone eating so loudly.

  C) Tina and Marie never saw anyone eating so loud.

  D) Tina and Marie had never seen someone eating so loud.

18. Choose the sentence that is written correctly.

  A) The holiday Cinco de Mayo, a Mexican-American tradition which celebrates the Mexican repulsion of the French occupation.

  B) The holiday Cinco de Mayo, a Mexican-American tradition, celebrates the Mexican repulsion of the French occupation.

  C) The holiday Cinco de Mayo, a Mexican-American celebration of the Mexican repulsion of the French occupation.

  D) The holiday Cinco de Mayo, a Mexican-American celebrating of the Mexican repulsion of the French occupation.

19. Choose the sentence that is written correctly.

  A) If you have questions about the schedule, please be seeing your counselor.

  B) If you have to ask the counselor your questions about the schedule.

  C) If you have questions about the schedule, please see your counselor.

  D) If you have a question about the schedule, be seeing your counselor.

20. Choose the sentence that is written correctly.

  A) The head zookeeper, who has been with the zoo for over twenty years, have agreed to set up a new enclosure for the elephants.

  B) Of all the elephants owned by the zoo, only some has been approved to move to the new enclosure.

  C) The rest of the elephants has been given to a well-respected rescue organization.

  D) The rescue organization, which takes in animals from zoos across the country, has agreed not to sell the elephants to another zoo.

21. Choose the word or words that best complete the sentence.

The children did not want to _____ their room after playing with all their toys.

  A) clean up

  B) clean over

  C) clear around

  D) clean off

22. Choose the sentence that is punctuated correctly.

  A) Make a study plan to learn the parts of the respiratory system, the muscles and the heart.

  B) Make a study plan to learn the: parts of the respiratory system, the muscles and the heart.

  C) Make a study plan to learn the parts of the respiratory system the muscles and the heart.

  D) Make a study plan to learn the parts: of the respiratory system, the muscles and the heart.

23. Choose the word or words that best complete the sentence.

Even though she is the _____ employee, Jessi finishes more projects than anyone else in the office.

  A) most new

  B) newer

  C) most newest

  D) newest

24. Choose the word or words that best complete the sentence.

Shawna is _____ than Alyssa at soccer, but Alyssa is a great basketball player.

A) more good

B) more better

C) better

D) the best

25. Choose the word or words that best complete the sentence.

The water company plans to build a new pipe to bring water _____ the community, improving the service.

A) from

B) out of

C) to

D) on

In researching animal adaptions, this research paper discusses the uses of bioluminescence, the ability of various ocean creatures and insects to create light. Use the body paragraph about hunting and the conclusion that follow to answer the corresponding questions.

Other animals use their bioluminescent abilities differently. On the head of an anglerfish, for example, is a long barb that lights up at the tip. The fish uses this light to lure smaller fish directly into its mouth. * In addition, bioluminescent animals may use their natural spotlight to seek out prey in dark places; still others use their light to surprise, disorient, and capture their meals.

Finally, some animals, like the firefly and some types of underwater crustaceans, use bioluminescence in their mating practices. Female syllid fireworms, for example, luminesce while swimming in circles in order to attract males of their species.

26. Between the third and fourth sentences (at the asterisk), the writer wants to add an additional detail about animals that use bioluminescence to hunt. Considering the tone and purpose of the passage, which of the following choices is most effective?

A) Even some sharks light up to attract prey!

B) If you ever have an opportunity to go deep-sea diving, you should take advantage of it and hope that you get to see an anglerfish in action.

C) The anglerfish may look scary, but it won't eat anything as large as a human.

D) These creatures are fascinating to watch in action.

27. The best placement for the underlined sentence is—

A) where it is now.

B) at the beginning of this paragraph.

C) at the end of the second paragraph.

D) after the first sentence of the fourth paragraph.

28. At the end, the writer wants to add a concluding sentence. Considering the tone and purpose of the passage, which choice is most appropriate?

A) Despite its initial intrigue, bioluminescence is far more common and less interesting than one might assume.

B) In conclusion, bioluminescence is an essential adaptation for many animals species, and we would be irresponsible to ignore it.

C) Boluminescent species are some of the most fascinating animals on our planet, so it is essential that we consider committing time and resources to preserving their natural habitats.

D) With its commonality among species and its variety of applications, bioluminescence is a fascinating topic that can enliven our senses and spark our curiosities about the natural world.

→ CONTINUE

29. Choose the word or words that best complete the sentence.

With majestic mountains, rolling prairies, breathtaking coastlines, and arctic expanses, the Canadian landscape _____ around the world for its beauty and diversity.

A) are famous

B) is famous

C) famous

D) were famous

30. Choose the word or words that best complete the sentence.

Despite studying for hours, Carlos could not _____ the math assignment.

A) figure out

B) figure on

C) figure around

D) figure through

ANSWER KEY

Mathematics

1.	D)	9.	C)	17.	D)	25.	D)
2.	C)	10.	B)	18.	C)	26.	C)
3.	C)	11.	A)	19.	C)	27.	B)
4.	C)	12.	A)	20.	D)	28.	B)
5.	C)	13.	B)	21.	D)	29.	C)
6.	A)	14.	B)	22.	D)	30.	C)
7.	D)	15.	A)	23.	A)		
8.	B)	16.	C)	24.	B)		

Reading

1.	A)	9.	B)	17.	B)	25.	A)
2.	B)	10.	D)	18.	A)	26.	B)
3.	D)	11.	A)	19.	A)	27.	D)
4.	B)	12.	C)	20.	B)	28.	A)
5.	D)	13.	A)	21.	D)	29.	D)
6.	C)	14.	B)	22.	A)	30.	D)
7.	D)	15.	B)	23.	A)		
8.	B)	16.	B)	24.	A)		

Writing

1.	A)	9.	C)	17.	B)	25.	C)
2.	C)	10.	A)	18.	B)	26.	A)
3.	B)	11.	C)	19.	C)	27.	A)
4.	A)	12.	A)	20.	D.	28.	D)
5.	A)	13.	C.	21.	A)	29.	B)
6.	D)	14.	C)	22.	A.	30.	A)
7.	D)	15.	D)	23.	D)		
8.	B)	16.	D)	24.	C)		